This **THIRD** volume of "**Fort Lauderdale 100**" with 100 **photographs** by internationally **known** NeoPopRealist artist **NADIA RUSS is** dedicated to the 'YACHTING Capital of the World' & 'Venice of America' - Fort Lauderdale. In 2011, Fort Lauderdale celebrated its **100**-year **anniversary**. Beautiful, **breathtaking**, unique, amazing, great, **unbelievable**, amusing, glamorous, **sunny**, sandy, fascinating and unforgettable, **Fort Lauderdale** was an **inspiration** for this collection made by Nadia RUSS in 2011. This **book** is **dedicated to** 52nd International Boat Show in Ft. Lauderdale, largest in its kind in the world, which took place October 27-31, 2011.

Эта (третья) книга фотографий художника Нади РУСС (Надежды Малолетневой) серии «Форт-Лодердейл 100» посвящена городу Форт-Лодердейлу и его Международной Выставке Яхт, самой популярной ежегодной выставке яхт в мире. В 2011, Форт-Лодердейл праздновал его годовщину - город вошел в 100-ый год его существования. Красивый и захватывающий дух, уникальный и удивительный, невероятно забавный, очаровательный, солнечный, песчаный, незабываемый - все это о городе Форт-Лодердейле, который был вдохновением для собрания этих фотографий, сделанных Надей РУСС во время Международной Выставки Яхт 27-31 октября 2011 года.

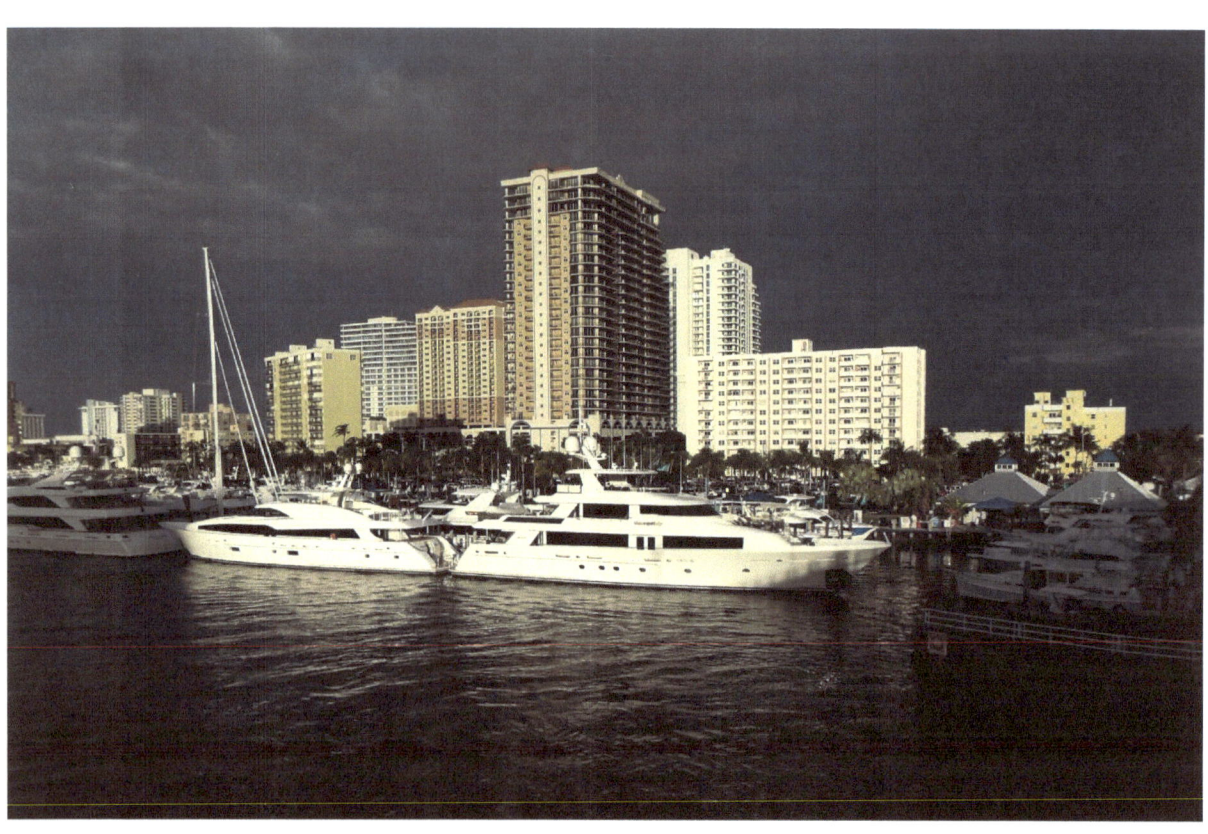

Fort Lauderdale

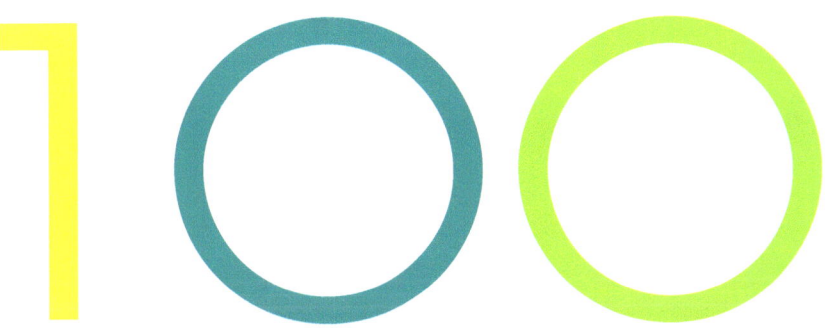

100

Yachting Capital

A Must-Have
Collector's Edition

NADIA RUSS
PHOTOGRAPHY

Fort Lauderdale 100
Yachting Capital

A Must-Have Collector's Edition

100 PHOTOGRAPHS

NADIA RUSS

NeoPopRealism**PRESS**

FOREWORD
by JOHN P. "JACK" SEILER
Mayor of the City of Fort Lauderdale

$\mathcal{A}$s Fort Lauderdale celebrates its historic 100th Birthday in 2011, we are truly a city that has come of age.

Incorporated on March 27, 1911, the City of Fort Lauderdale is embraced by the Atlantic Ocean, Intracoastal Waterway, New River, and an intricate system of inland waterways and canals, all of which give rise to the City's designation as the *Venice of America.*

As the seventh largest city in Florida and the largest city in Broward County, Fort Lauderdale is the heart of a robust, dynamic, high-growth region that is home to a diverse range of industries, including marine, tourism, manufacturing, finance, insurance, real estate, high technology, avionics/aerospace, and film and television production.

As the Yachting Capital of the World, Greater Fort Lauderdale's marine industry now accounts for more that 134,000 jobs and generates $13.6 billion in total economic impact. The area boasts hundreds of miles of waterways, state-of the art marinas, outstanding marine manufacturing and repair facilities, and is home to the Fort Lauderdale International Boat Show, the world's largest international boat show with an annual economic impact of more that $500 million.

With sparkling beaches, crystal blue waters and an abundance of sunshine, Greater Fort Lauderdale remains the destination of choice for millions of domestic and international visitors. The tourism industry continues to thrive, hosting more than 10 million visitors annually who spend in excess of $8.5 billion.

The renaissance of downtown Fort Lauderdale began with Riverwalk, a massive and historic capital improvement program that brought millions of dollars of investment to the heart of downtown. The picturesque Riverwalk serves as the cornerstone of the City's arts, science, cultural, and historic district, and features the Broward Center for the Performing Arts, Museum of Discovery and Science, Museum of Art, and Fort Lauderdale History Center.

Downtown's Las Olas Boulevard has gained international acclaim as Fort Lauderdale's centerpiece of fashion, fine dining, and entertainment. The City's dynamic central business district features major companies, government offices, federal and county courthouses, and educational institutions including Broward College, Florida Atlantic University, Florida International University, and Nova Southeastern University.

Major investments in assets and amenities downtown and along the beach have served as a catalyst for establishing the City of Fort Lauderdale as a world-class international business center and one of the most desirable locations for new, expanding, or relocating businesses.

With a broad range of global business opportunities, access to domestic and international markets, a pro business government, low labor rates, a well-educated and diverse work force,

a variety of housing options, a low tax burden, and an array of business assistance and incentive programs, the City of Fort Lauderdale is an unbeatable location where both large and small businesses can prosper.

Our outstanding business assets are matched only by our exceptional quality of life. Fort Lauderdale offers a semi-tropical climate, rich natural beauty, and an array of cultural, entertainment, and educational amenities.

From the world-famous Fort Lauderdale Beach to the quaint Riverwalk, from the bustling Himmarshee Village to the chic ease of Las Olas Boulevard, Fort Lauderdale is a city that offers premiere opportunities for sight seeing, shopping, dining, leisure and recreation.

Outdoor activities abound with golf, tennis, boating, scuba, snorkeling, fishing, and sailing. The area is home to professional teams in every major sport and hosts world-class swimming and diving events at the Fort Lauderdale Aquatic Complex and International Swimming Hall of Fame.

As the City moves forward, we will continue to work in partnership with our most important asset - our citizens - to ensure a bright future for ourselves, our children and future generations.

By remaining focused on our vision, we are confident that we can enhance the unique characteristics that make the City of Fort Lauderdale an outstanding place to live, work, visit, play and raise a family.

INTRODUCTION
by NADIA RUSS

Fort Lauderdale is an amazing city. I discovered Fort Lauderdale for myself in the late 90s, when I came on a cruise ship from the Bahamas. When I arrived on this land for the first time, the only word I could find was "WOW!" And now, more than ten years later, I still have this "WOW!" every time I see A1A, or Las Olas, or Sea Breeze Boulevard. During my first visit, I couldn't imagine that one day I would live in Fort Lauderdale; it seemed unreal. But it's mesmerizing, powerful beauty attracts me again and again. And now, New York City and Fort Lauderdale have almost equal places in my heart. Someone said that "people can get used to everything." It is not true, I cannot get used to the uniqueness and beauty I see in Fort Lauderdale: the amazing tropical plants, fascinating and polished A1A beach with its Atlantic Ocean, glamorous Las Olas Boulevard with its Isles, bridges and big yachts and homes at every corner, and small shops and restaurants that give you the feeling of comfort as if you were at home. This year, the city celebrates its 100 year anniversary. In January, I decided to make a photography book, dedicated to it. The photographs you will see here are made during 52nd International Fort Lauderdale Boat Show. This is the 3rd volume of the book "Fort Lauderdale 100".

ВВЕДЕНИЕ НАДИ РУСС
(Надежды Малолетневой)

Форт-Лодердейл удивительный город. Для себя я обнаружила Форт-Лодердейл в конце 90-ых, когда прибыла сюда с круизом с Багам. Тогда я ступила на его землю со словами: "НИЧЕГО СЕБЕ!". И теперь, больше чем десять лет спустя, я по-прежнему восхищюсь этим городом, и чувство "WOW!" возникает во мне каждый раз когда я вижу A1A, Las Olas бульвар... В течение моего первого посещения я даже не могла вообразить, что однажды я буду жить в Форт-Лодердейле, это казалось нереальным. Но его гипнотизирующая, мощная красота привлекает меня снова и снова. И теперь Нью-Йорк и Форт-Лодердейл имеют почти равноценное место в моем сердце. Кто-то сказал, что "люди привыкают ко всему." Это не верно. Я не могу привыкнуть к той уникальной красоте, которую вижу в Форт-Лодердейле. Это удивительные тропические растения и пляж на А1А с захватывающим дух Атлантическим океаном, очаровательный Las Olas Бульвар с его островами, большие дома с яхтами на каждом углу, маленькие магазинчики и рестораны, которые дают чувство комфорта, как будто вы дома.

В этом году город празднует его 100-летнюю годовщину. В январе я решила издать книгу, посвященную этой дате, с фотографиями, изображающими Форт-Лодердейл. Фотографии, которые вы видите здесь, сделаны в течение 52-ой Международной выставки Яхт в Форт-Лодердейле. Это 3-я часть книги "Форт-Лодердейл 100".

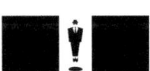

Fort Lauderdale 100
Yachting Capital

NADIA RUSS

Photography

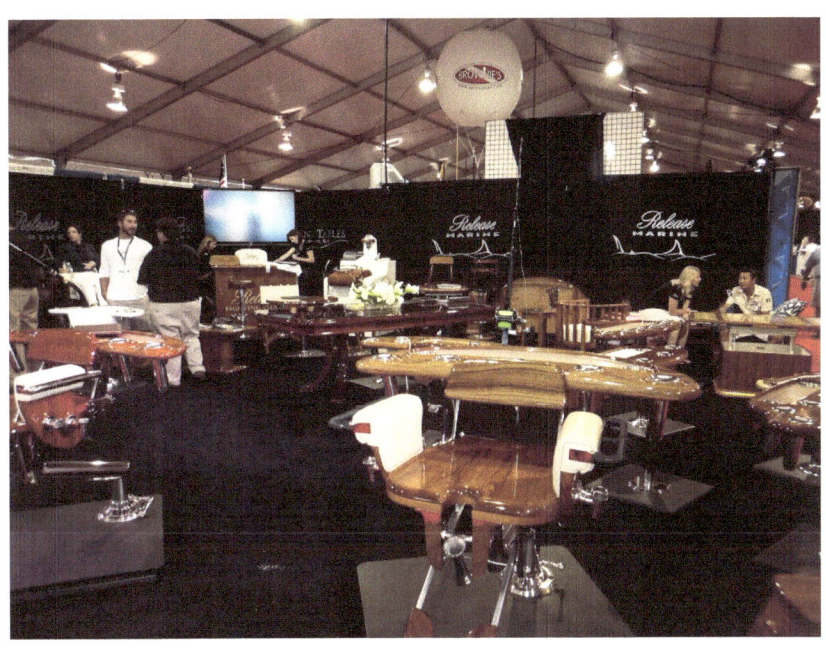

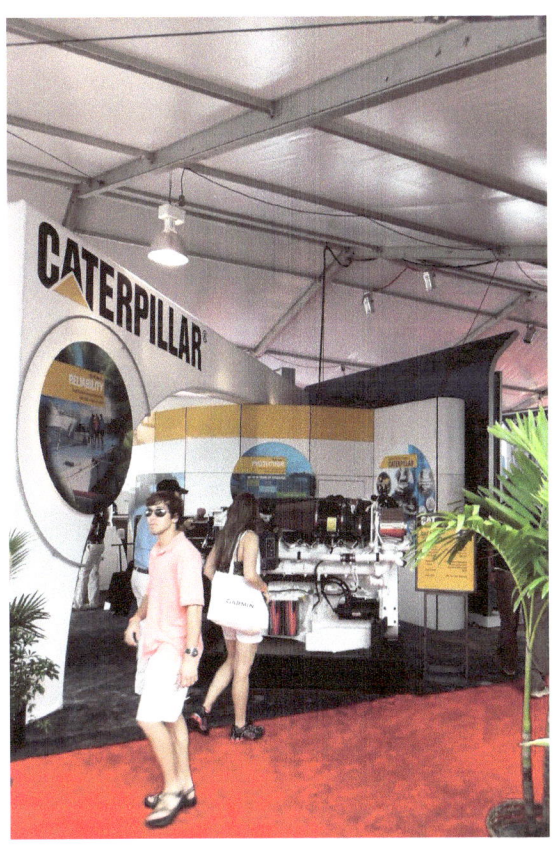

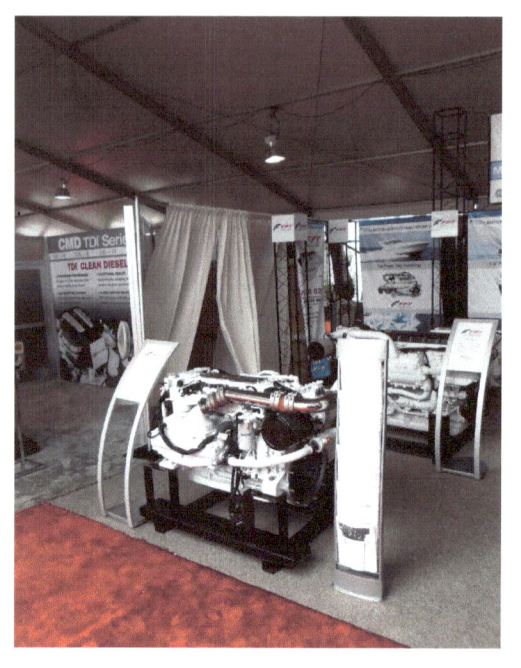

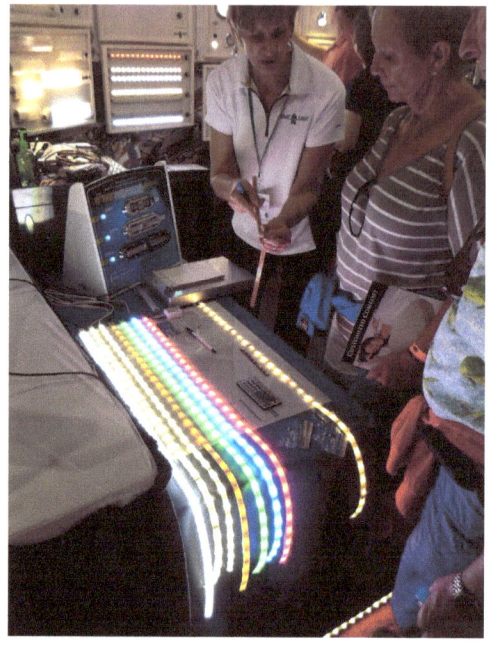

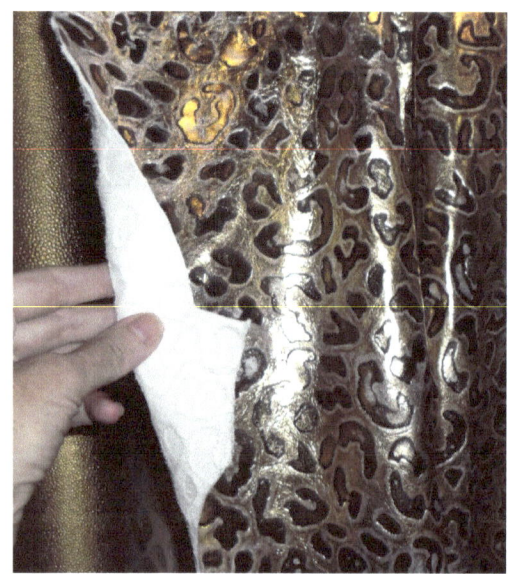

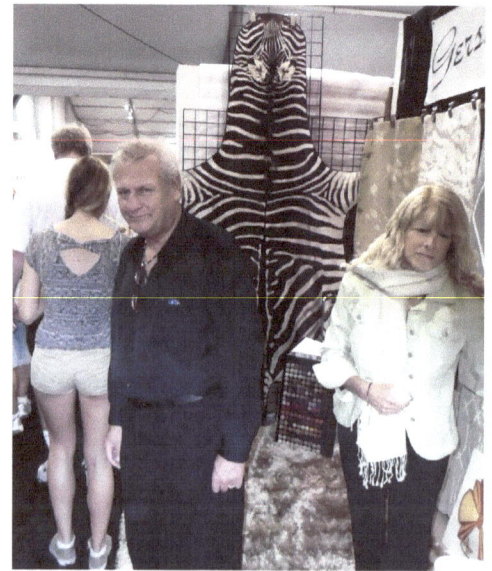

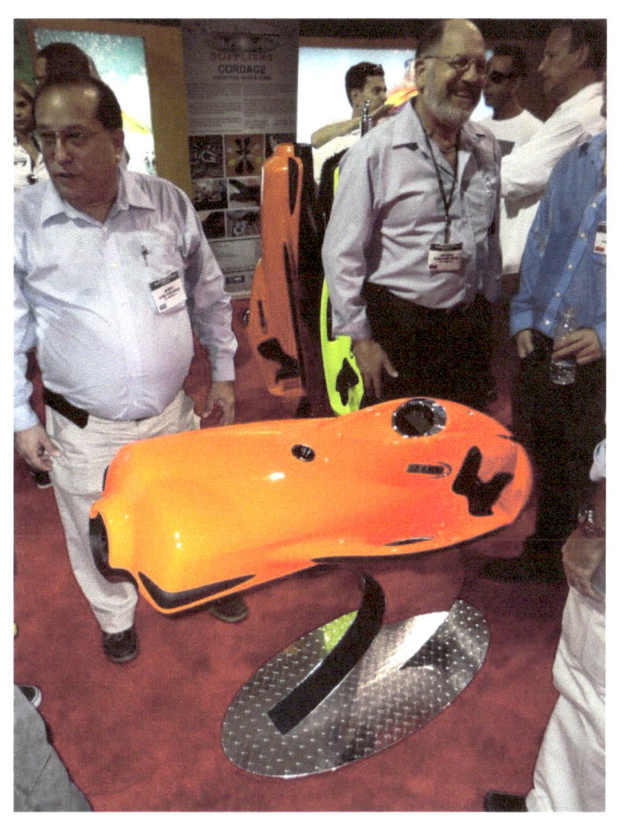

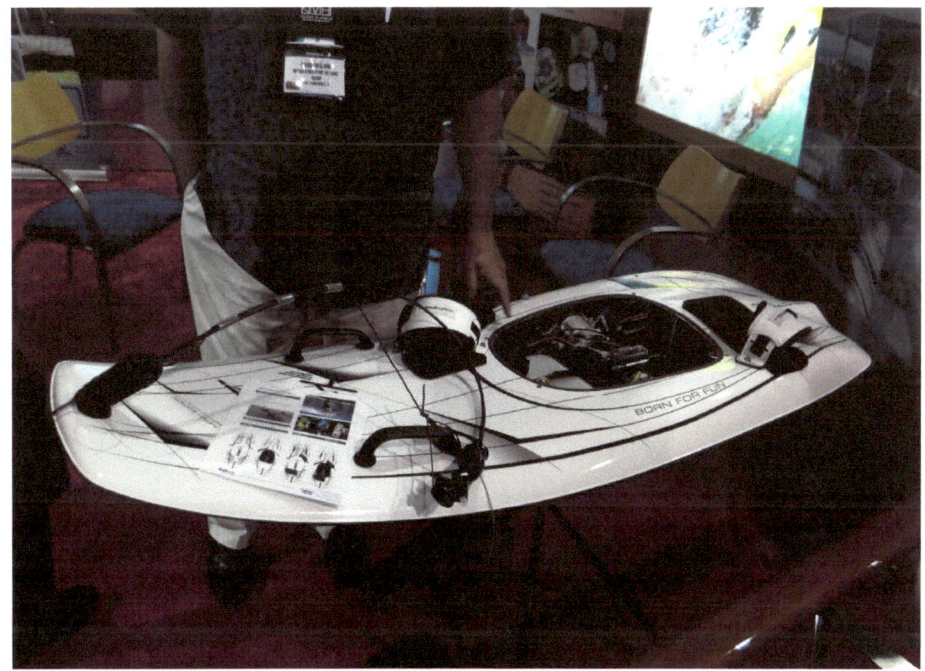

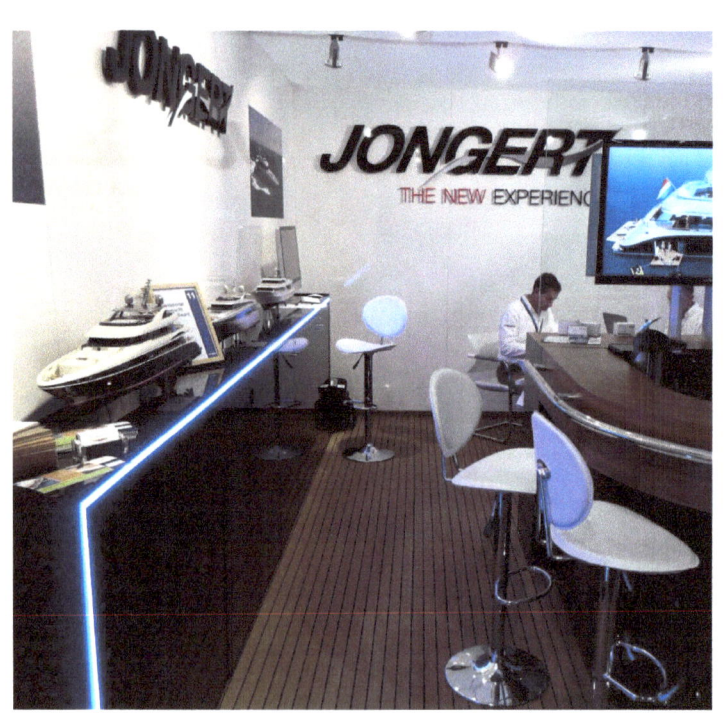

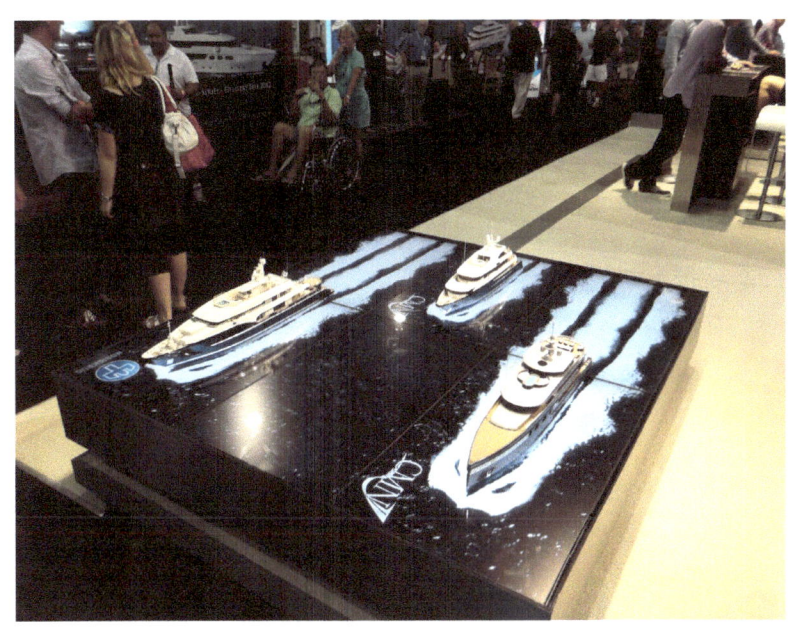

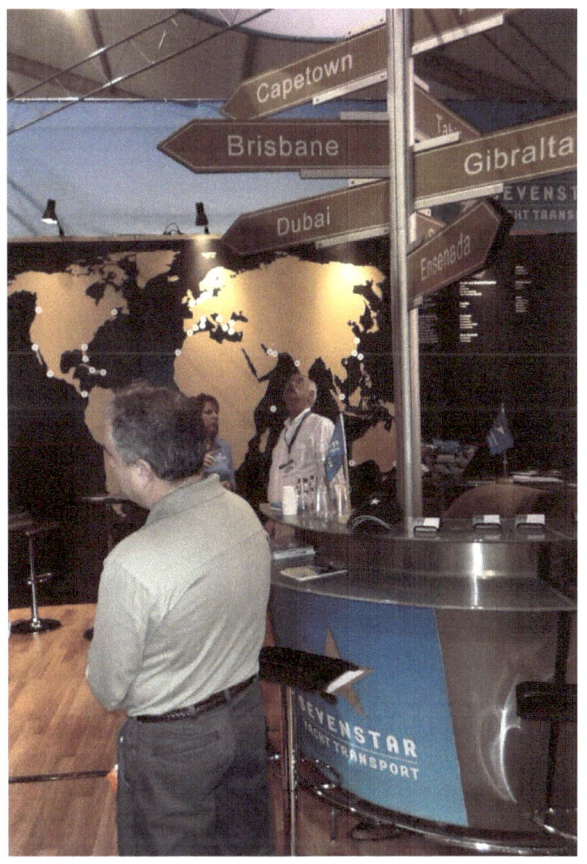

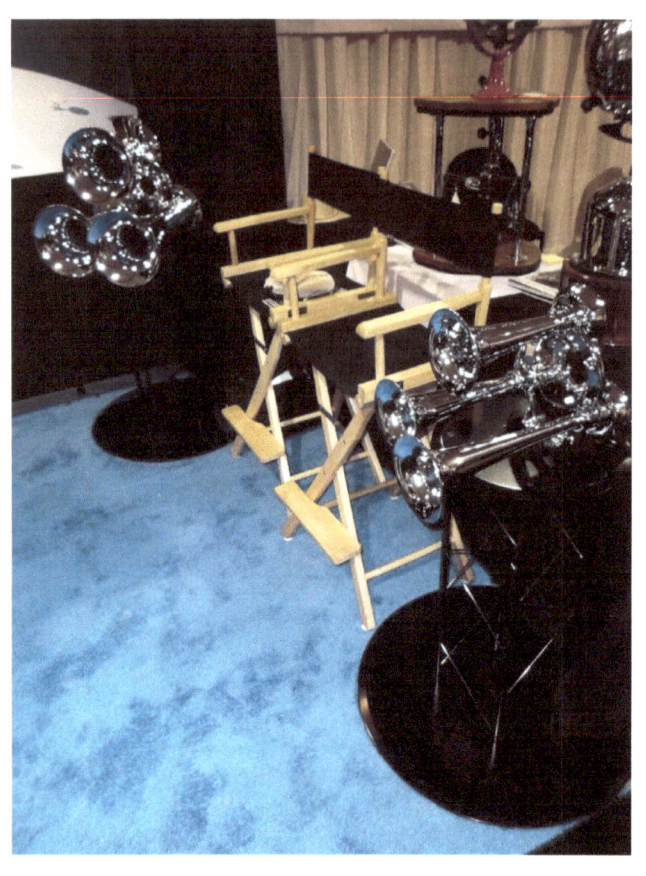

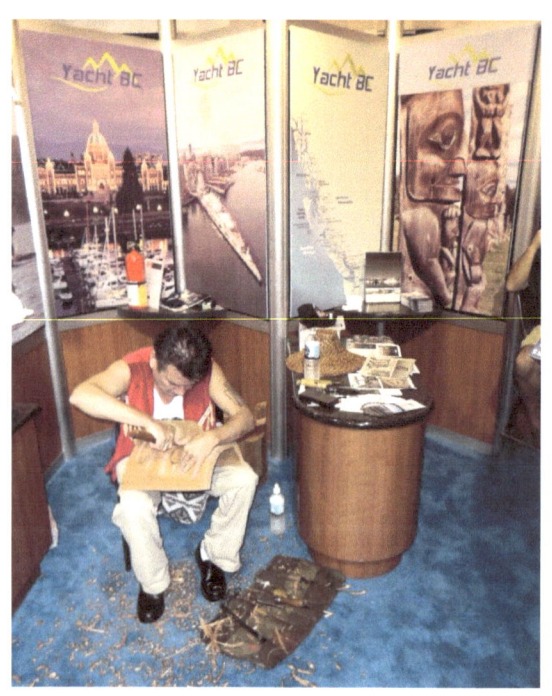

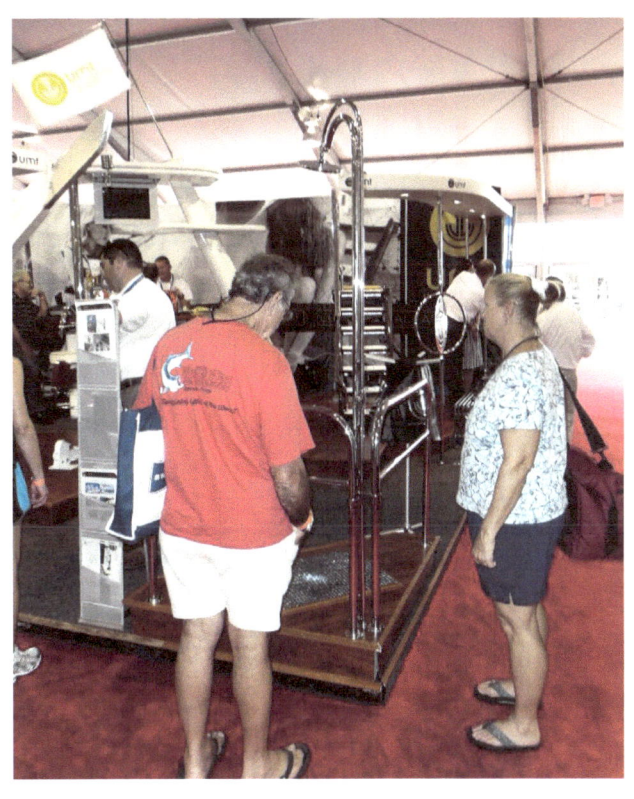

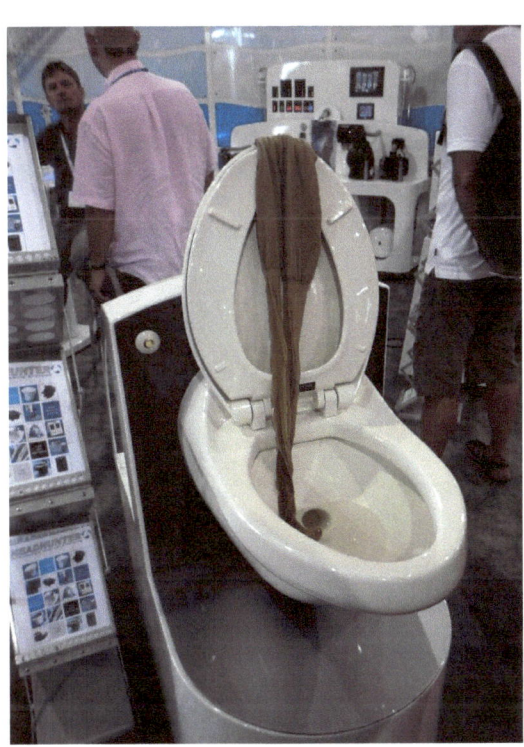

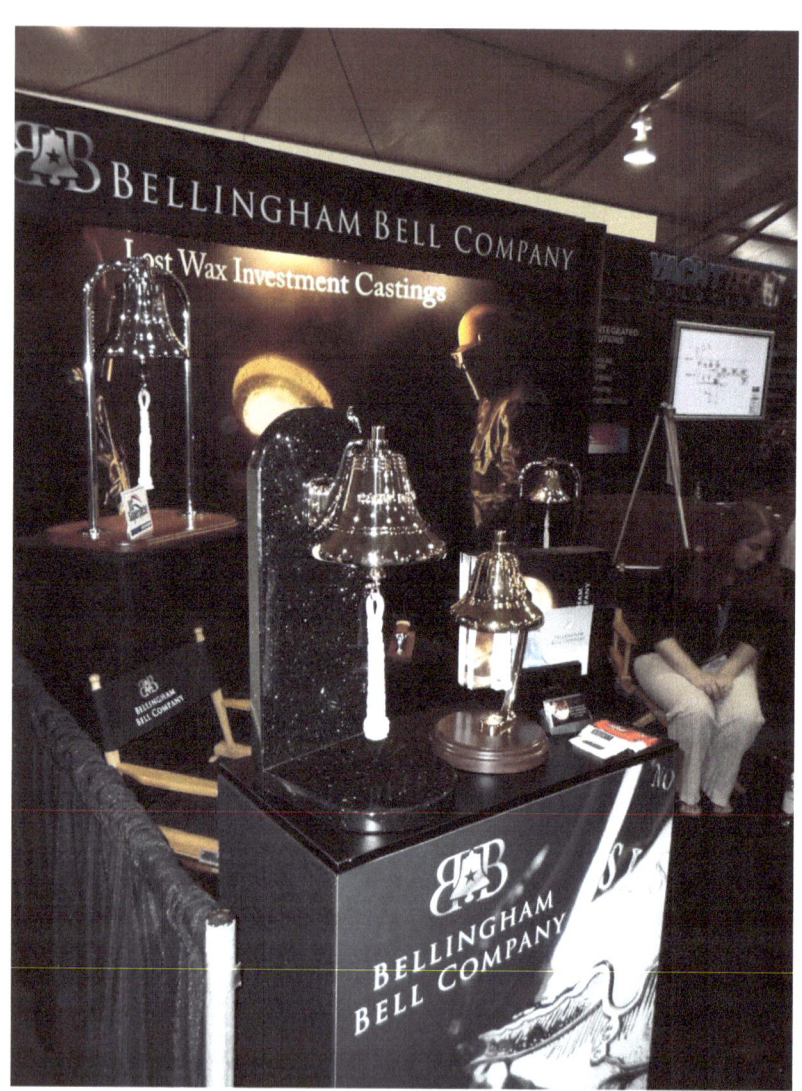

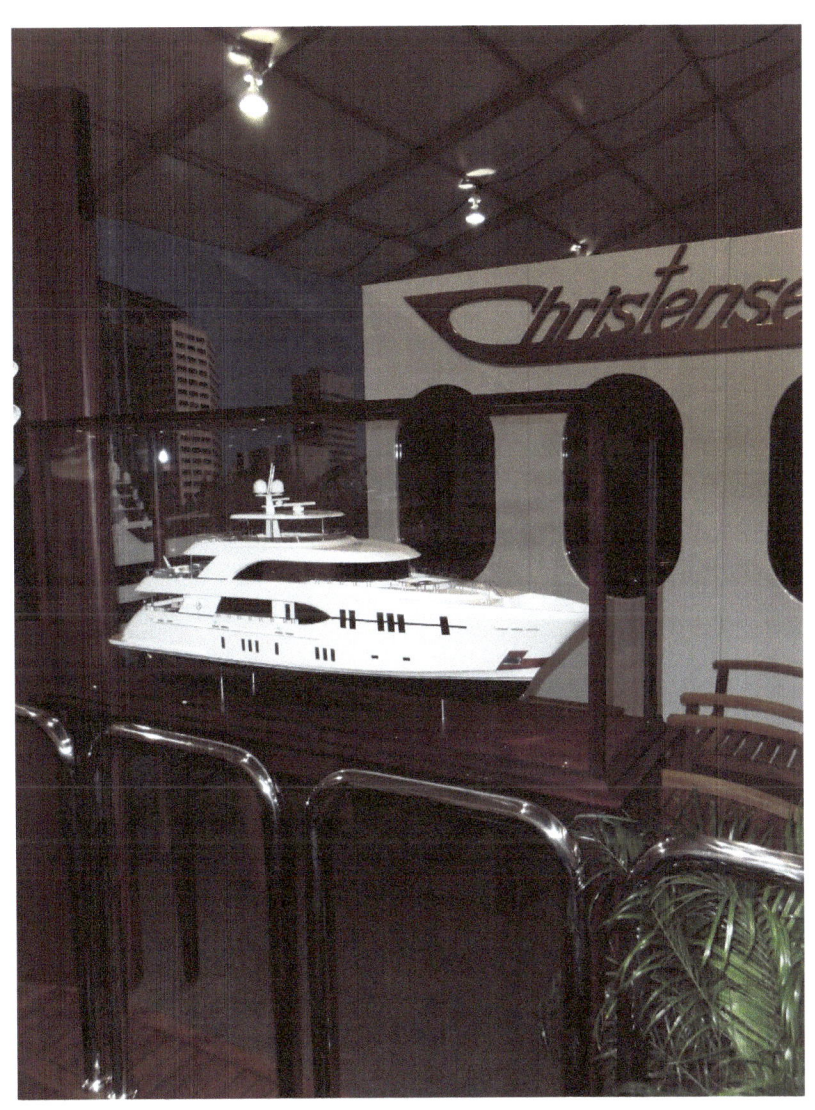

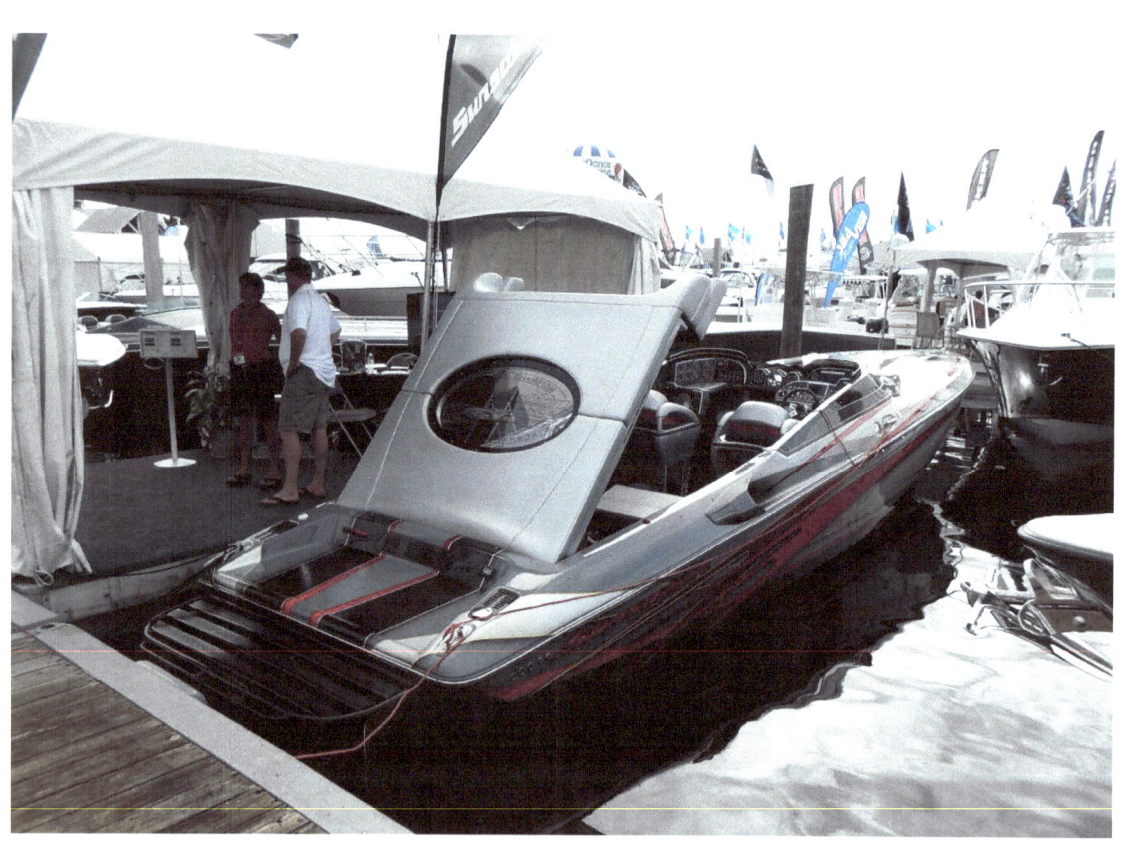

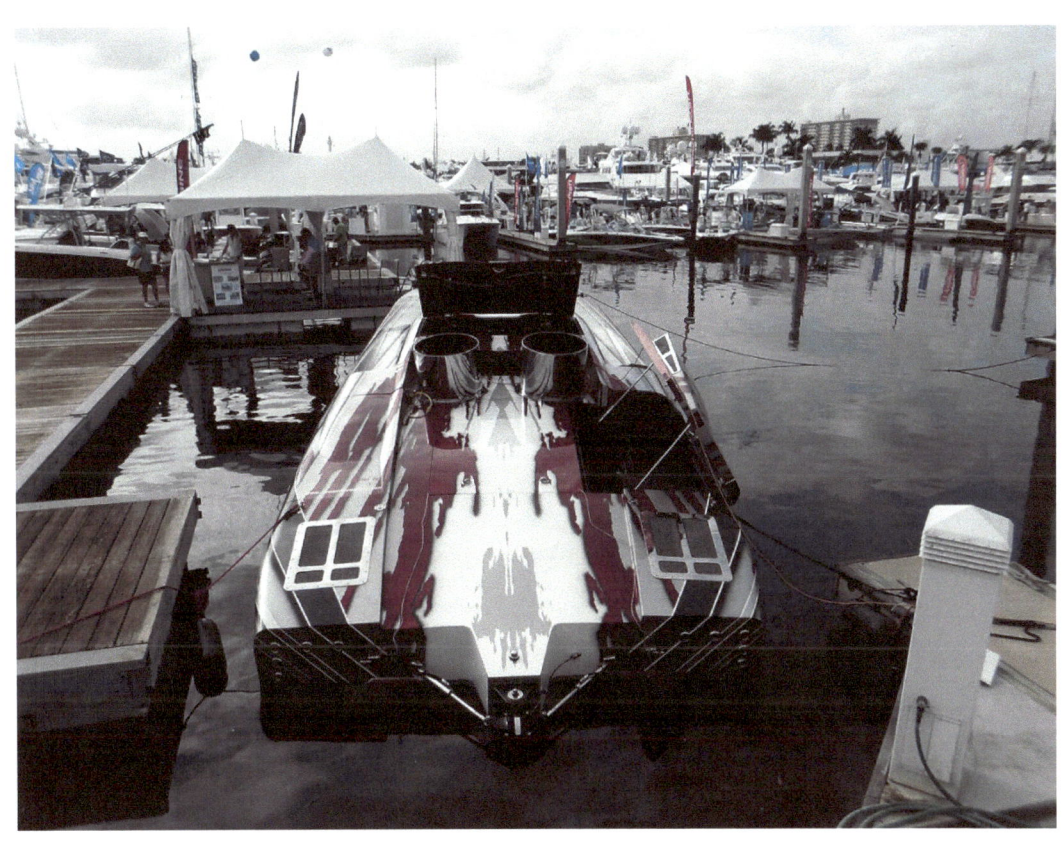

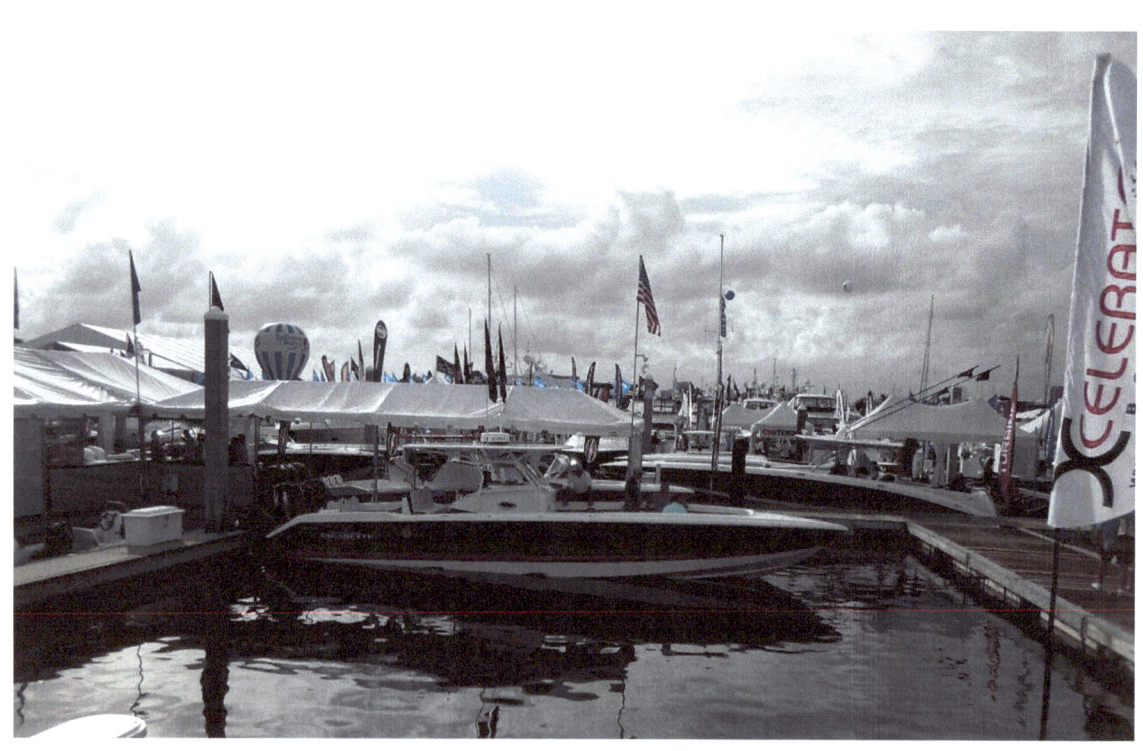

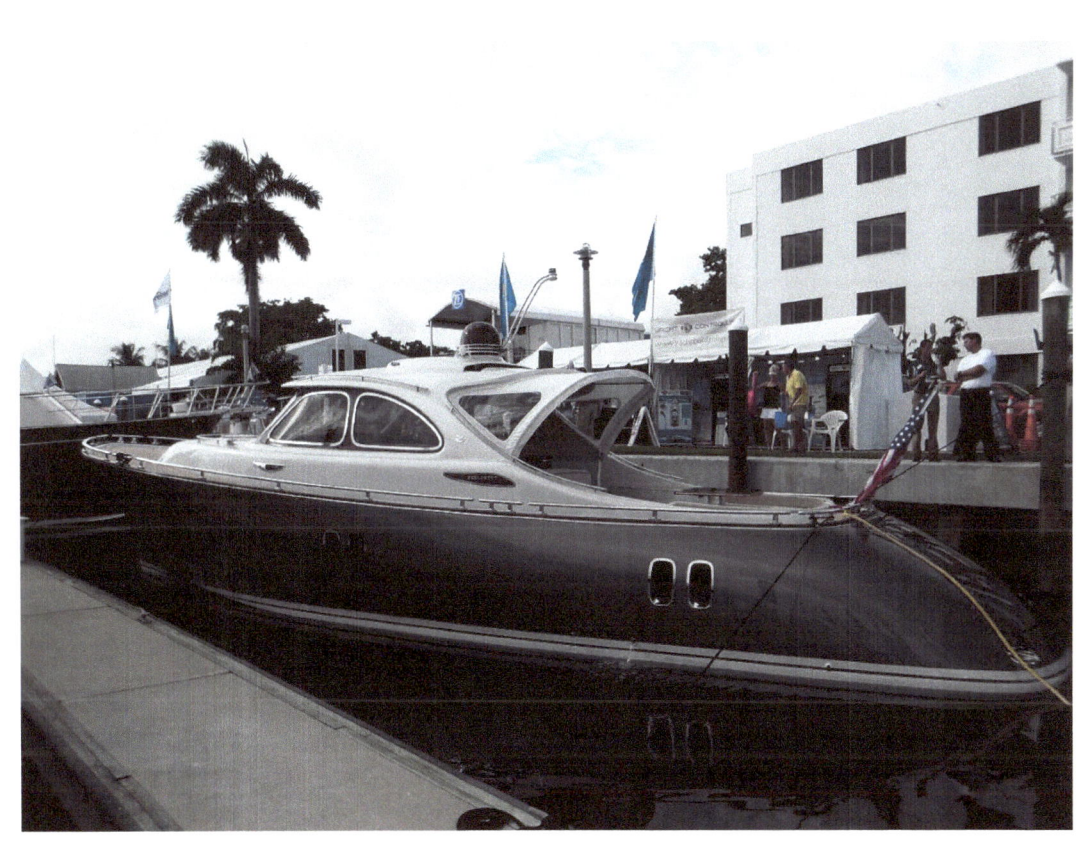

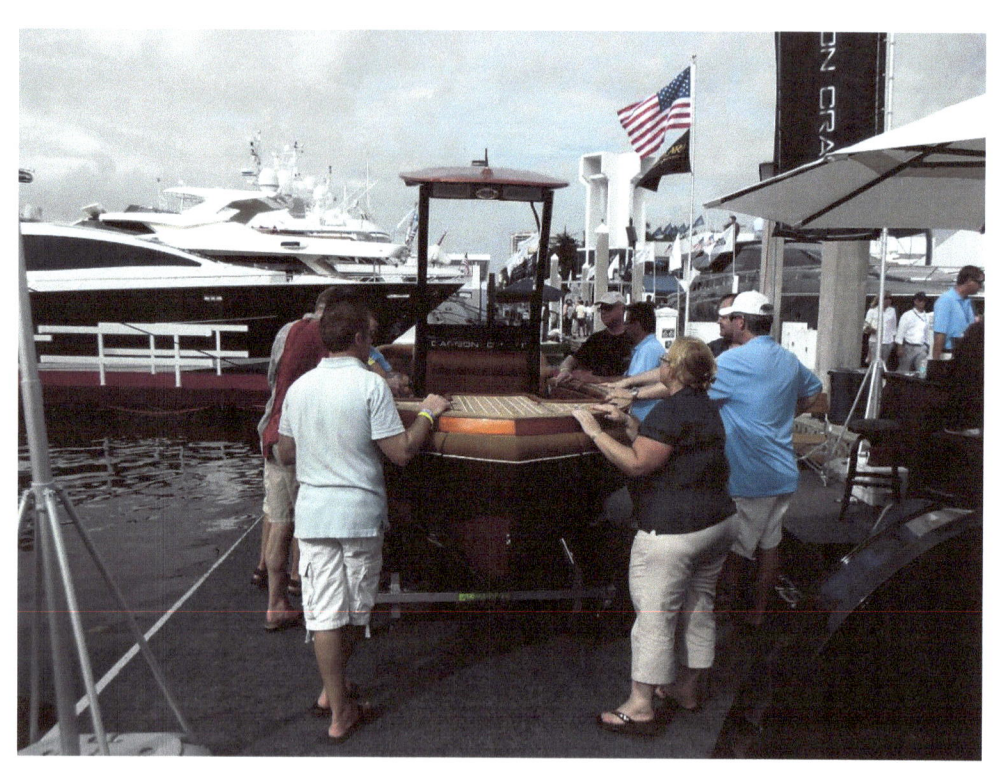

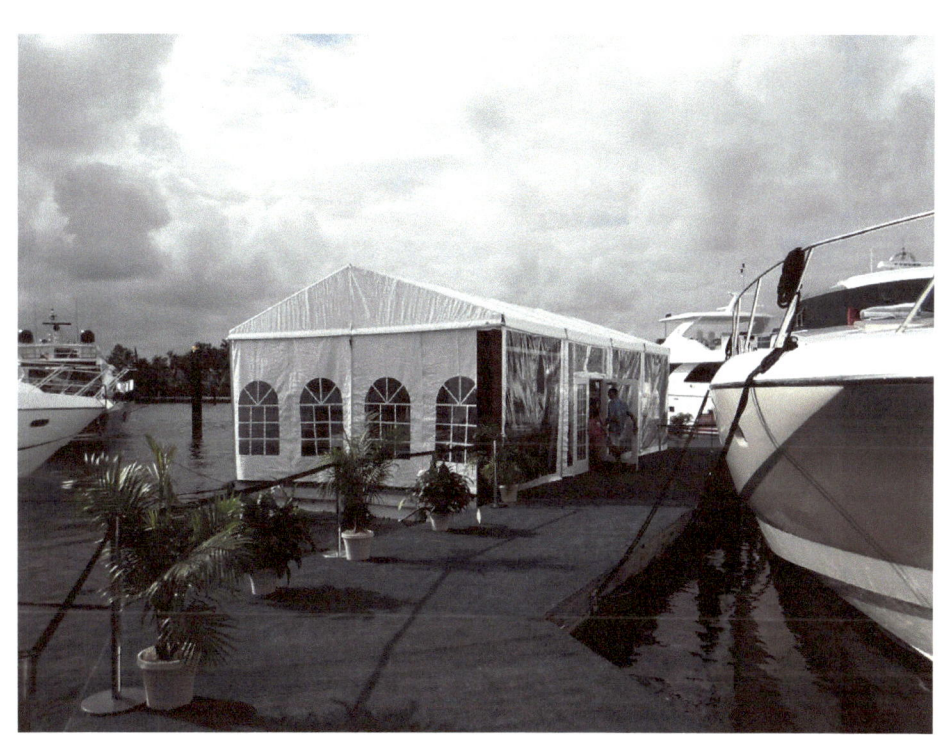

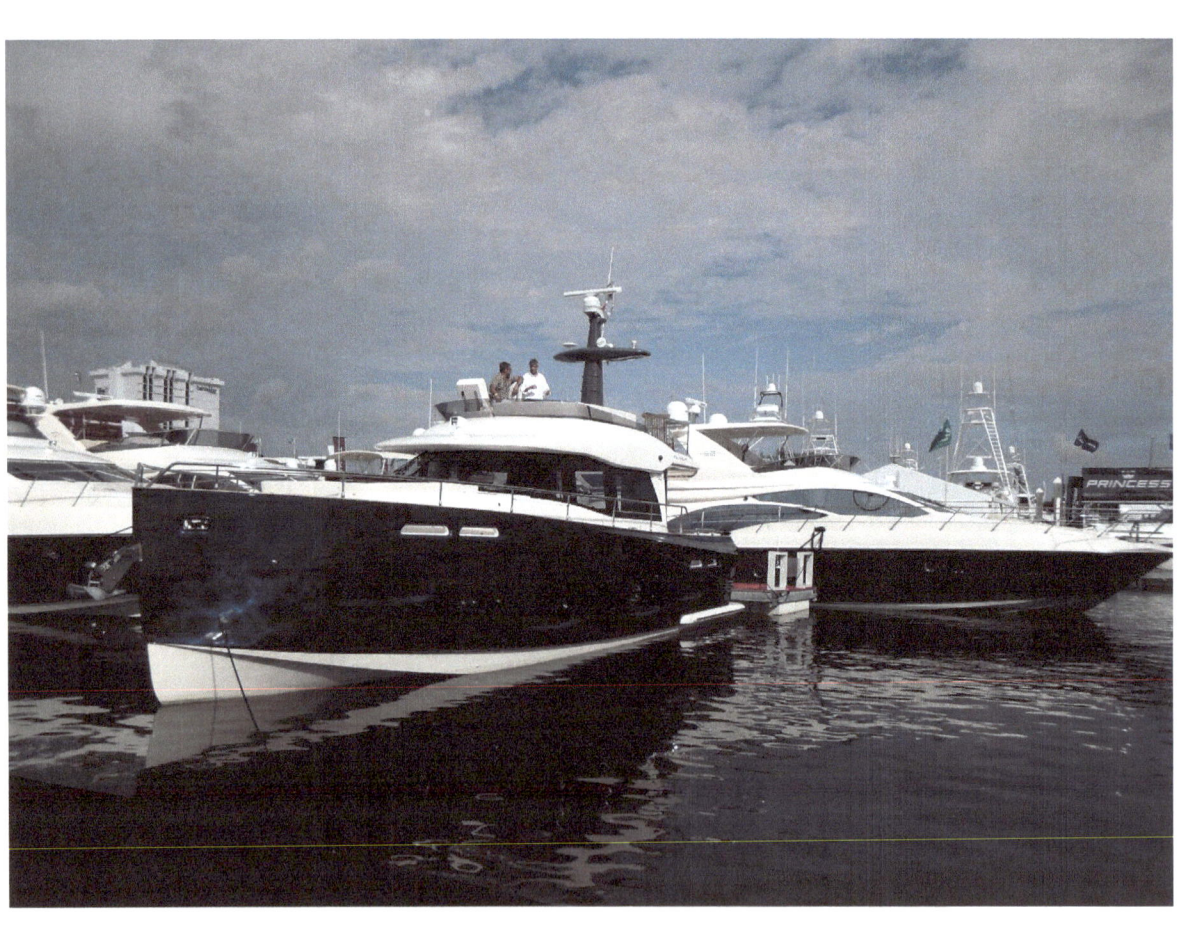

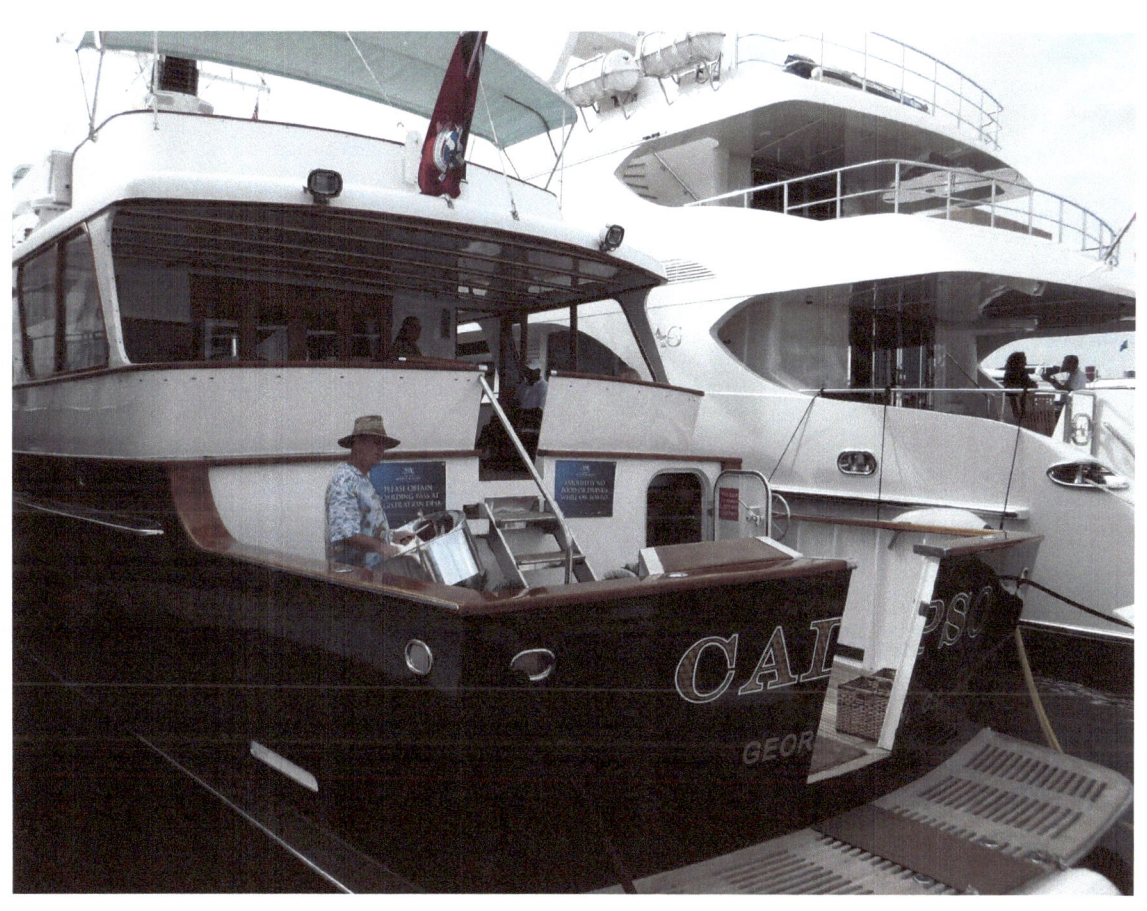

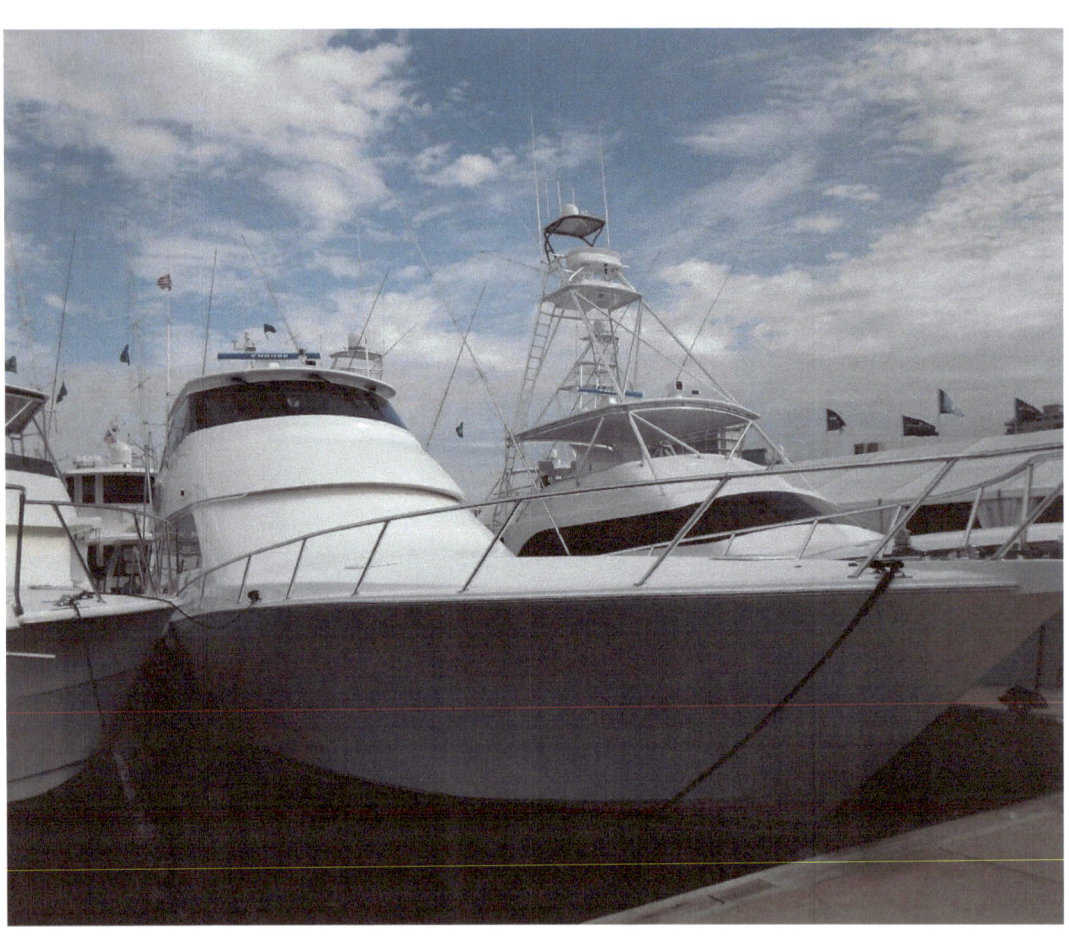

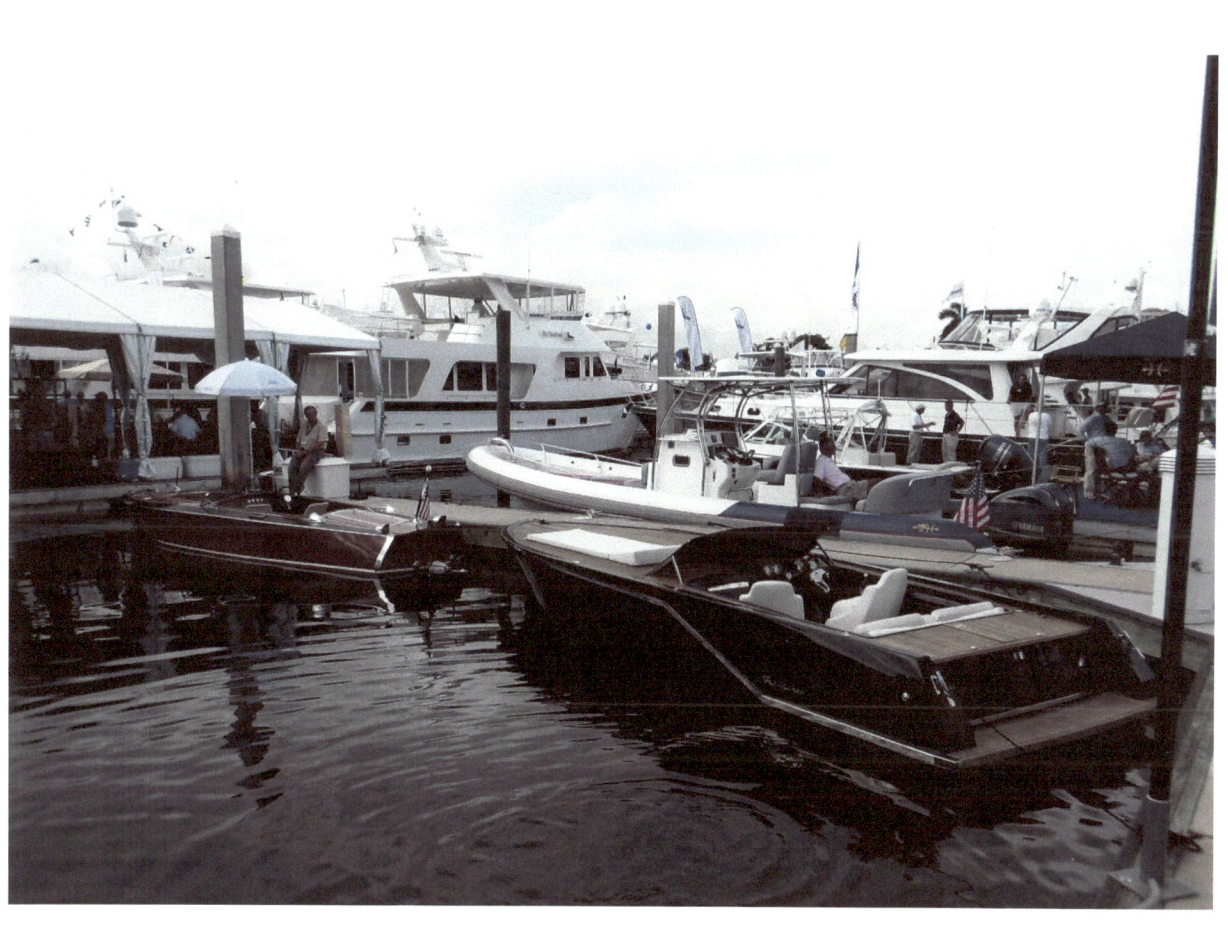

fort lauderdale 100: yachting capital

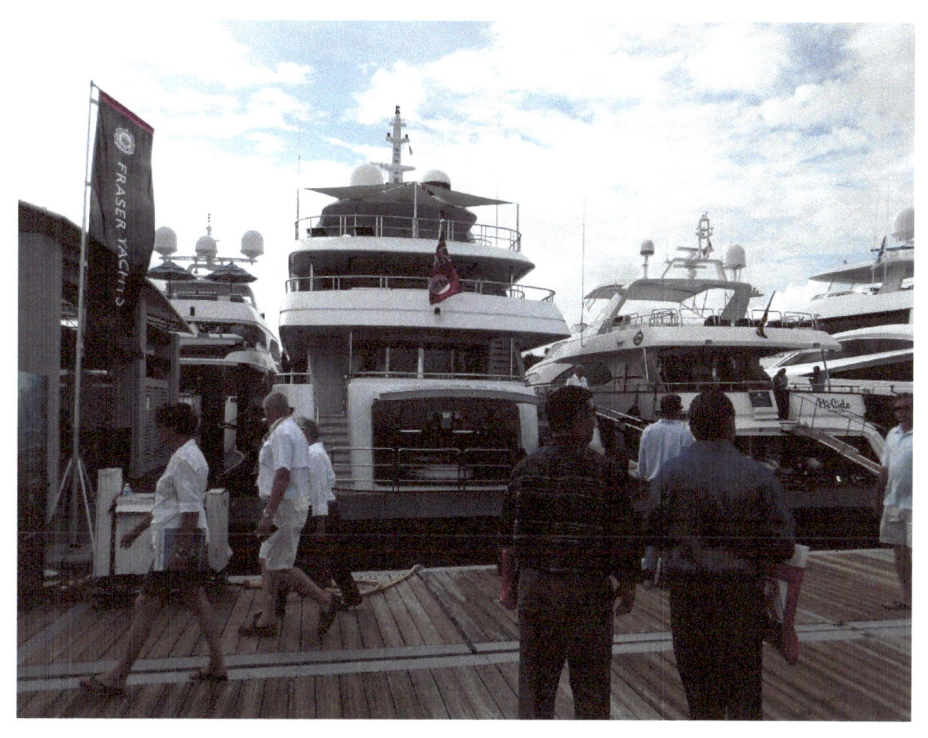

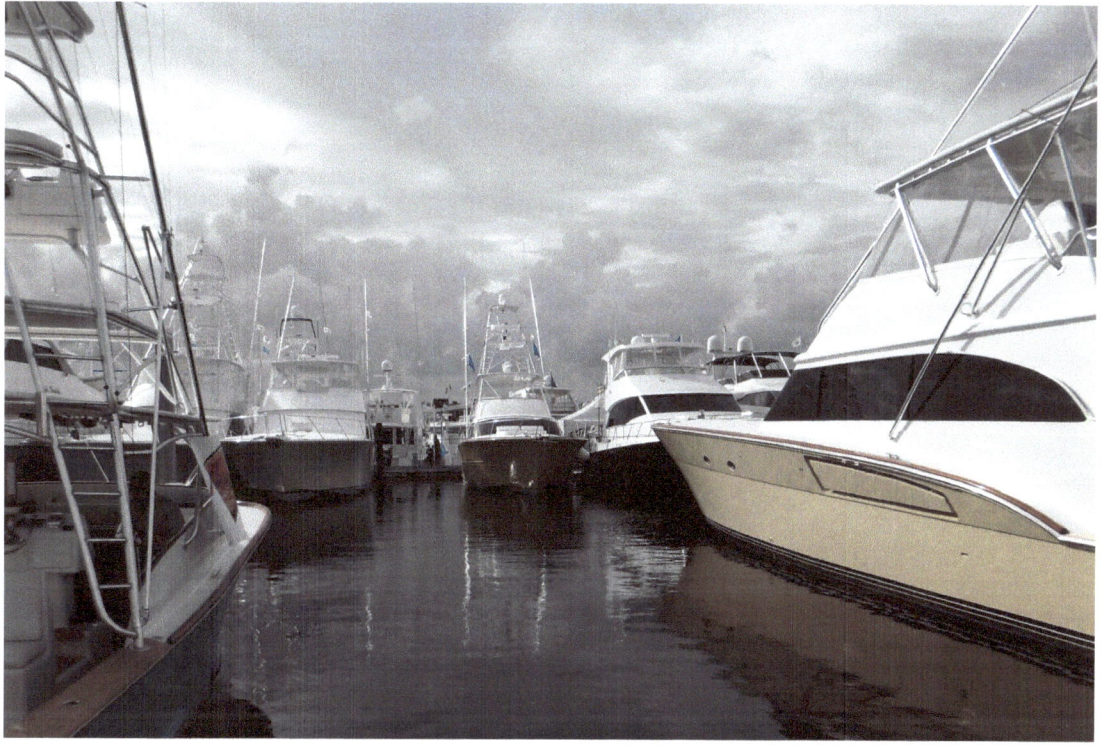

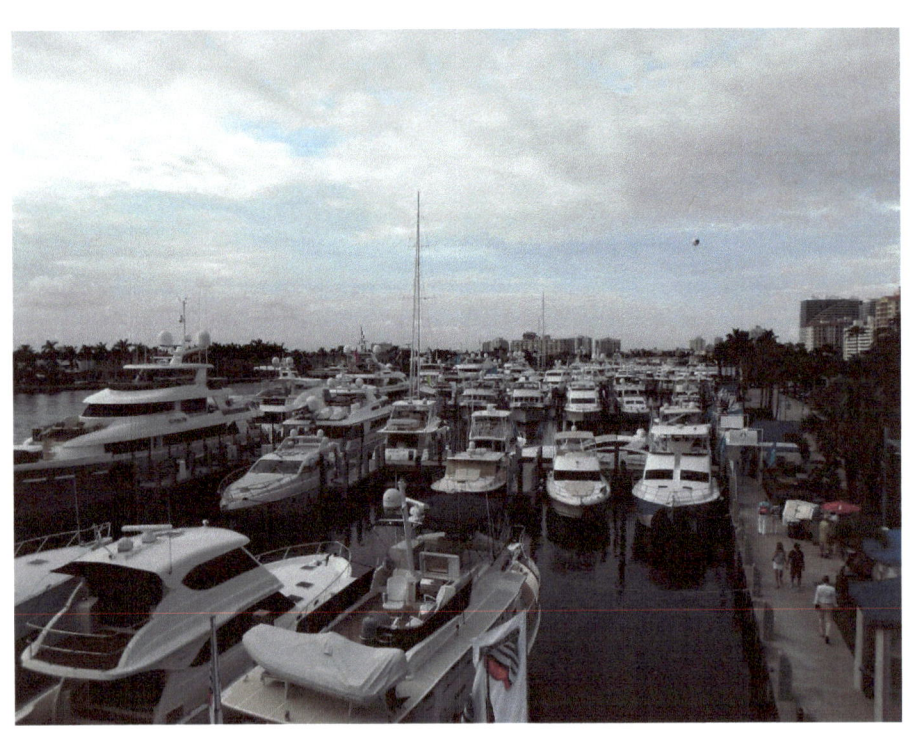

Fort Lauderdale 100

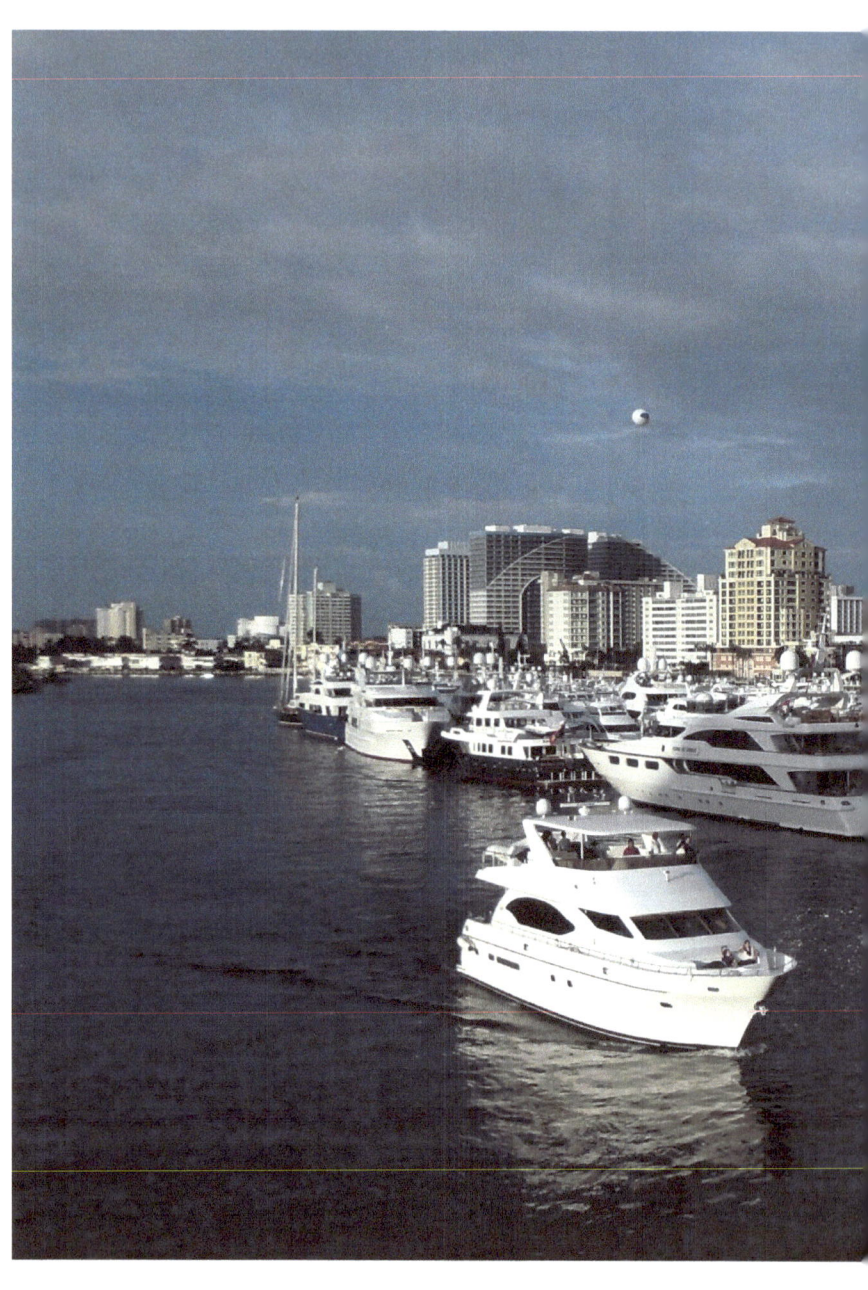

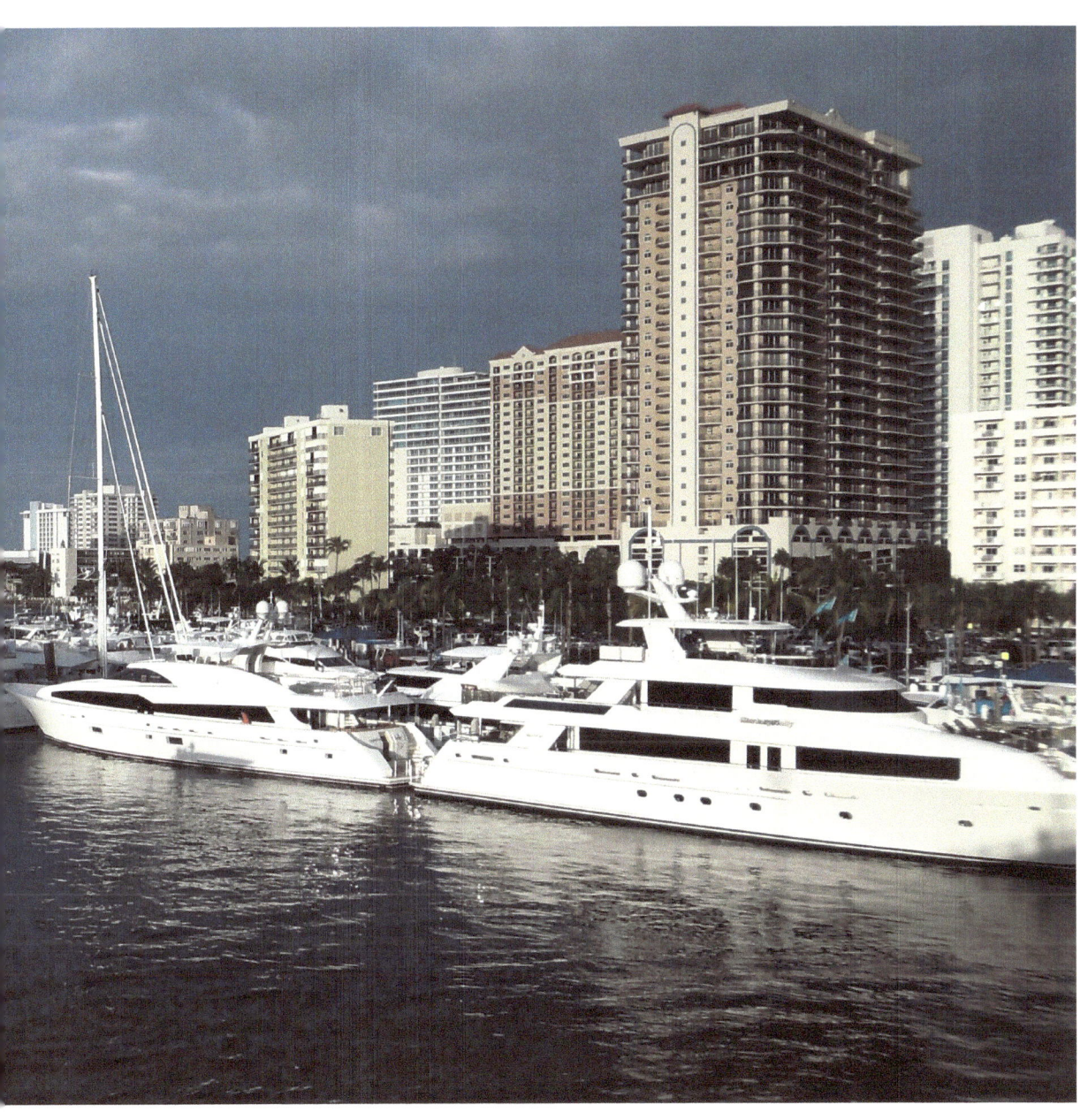

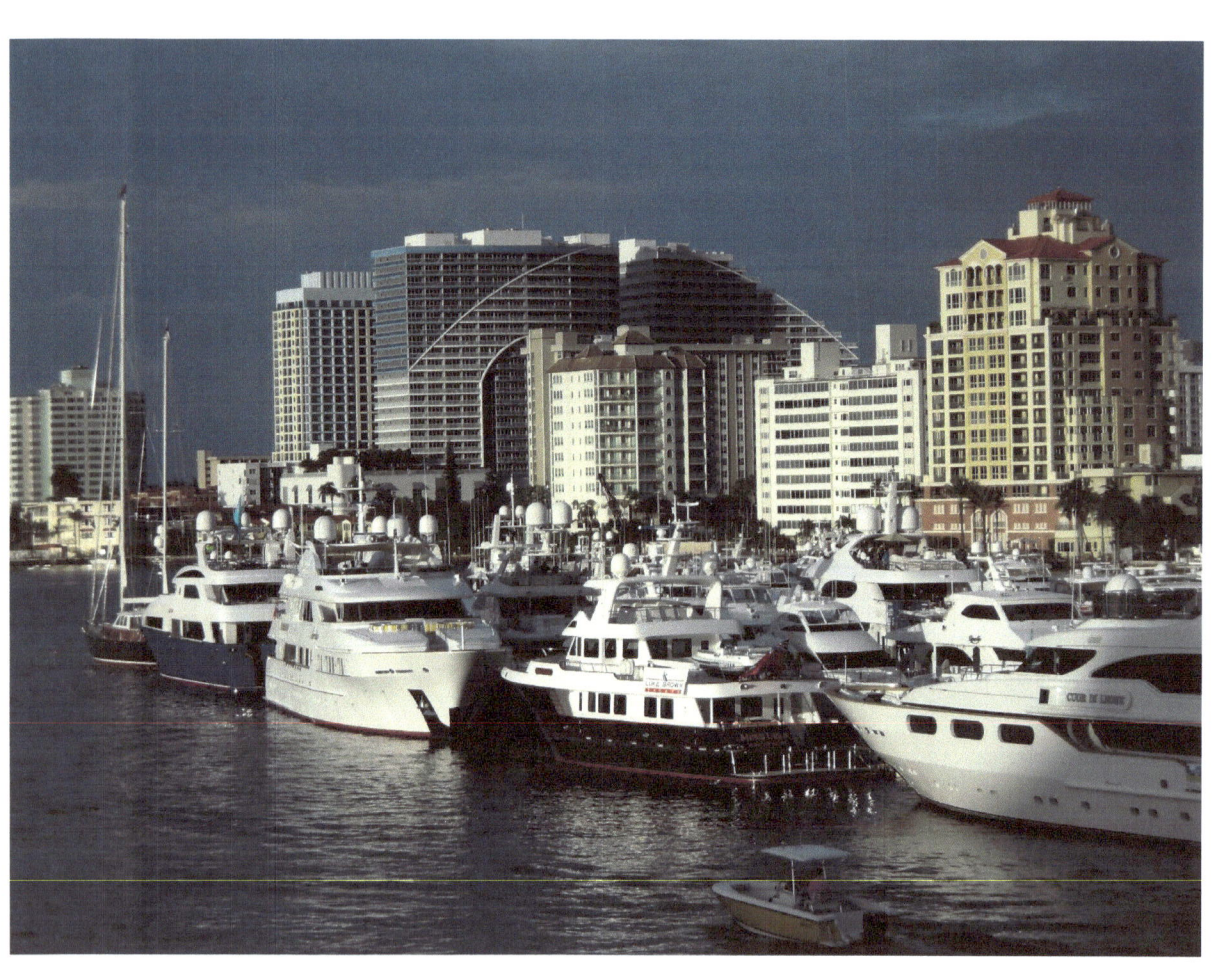

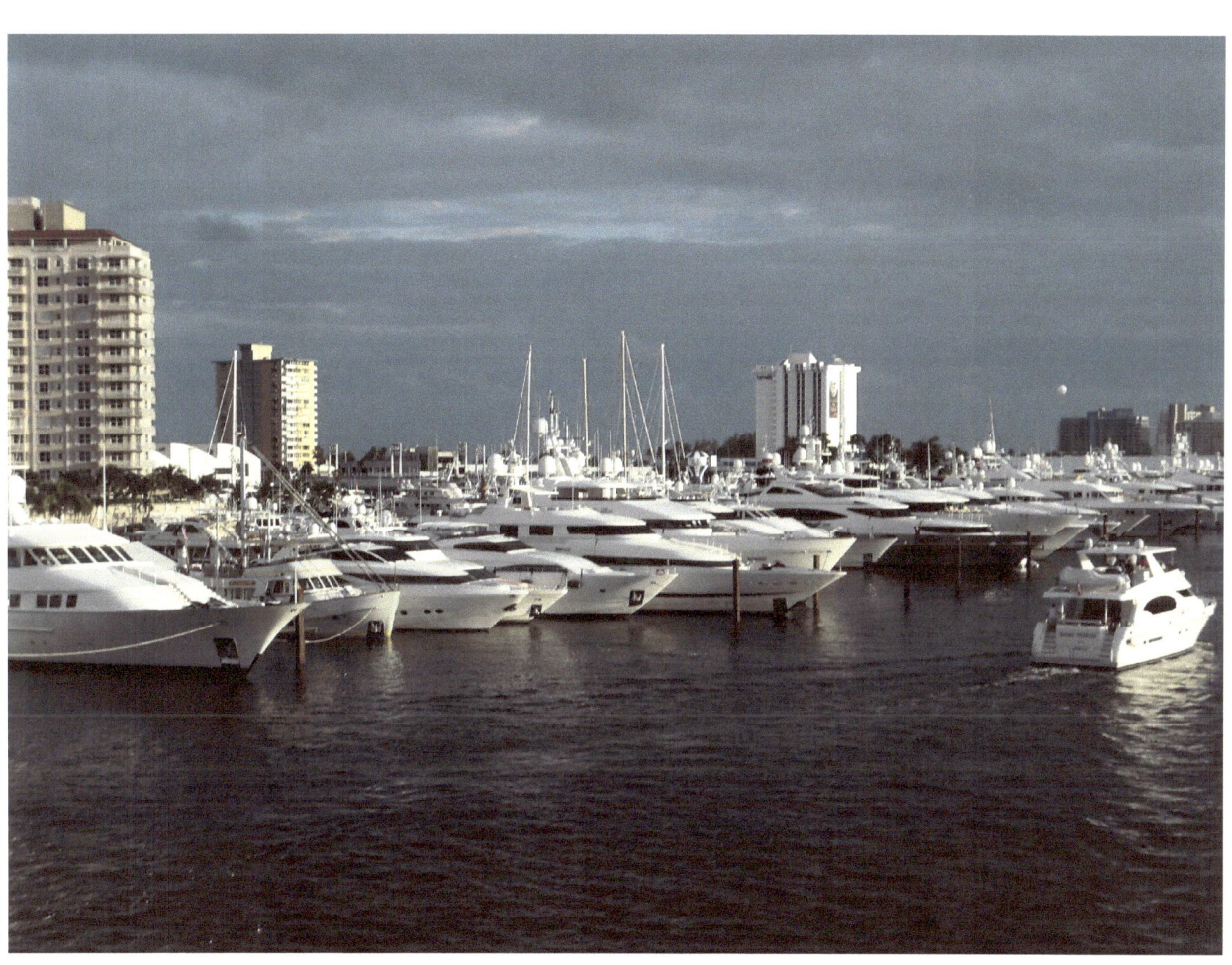

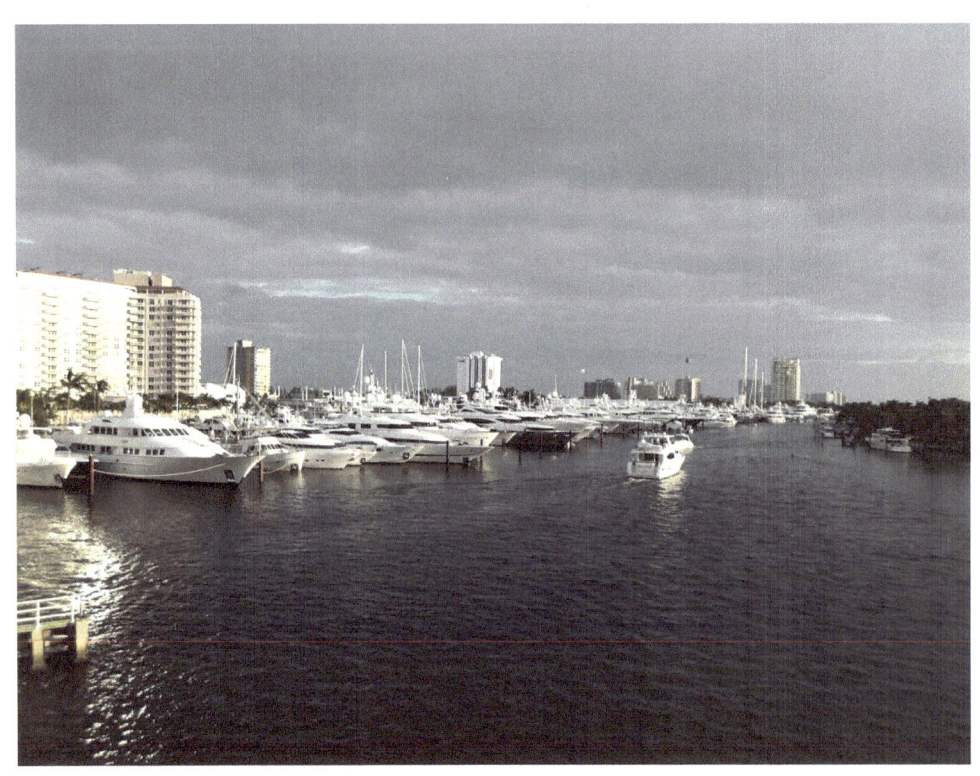

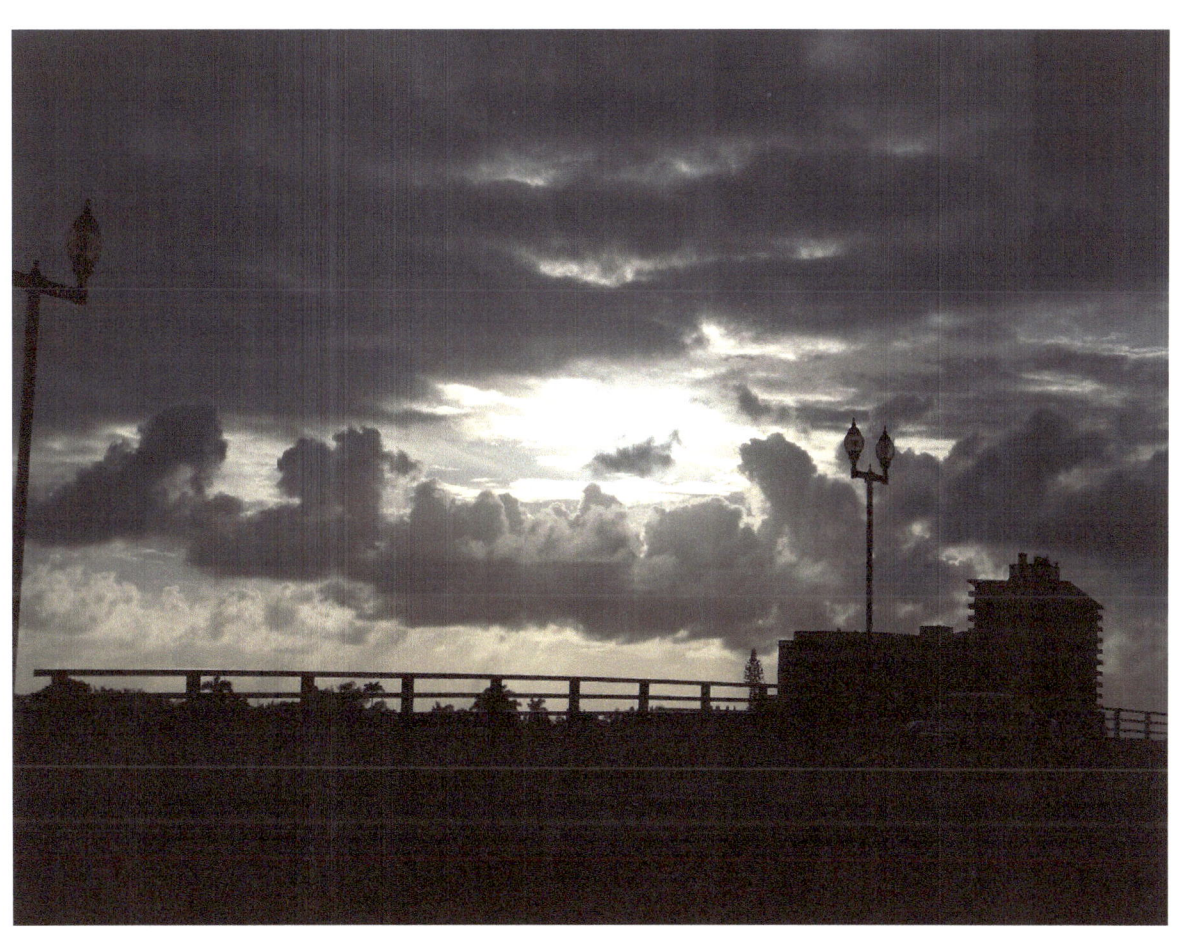

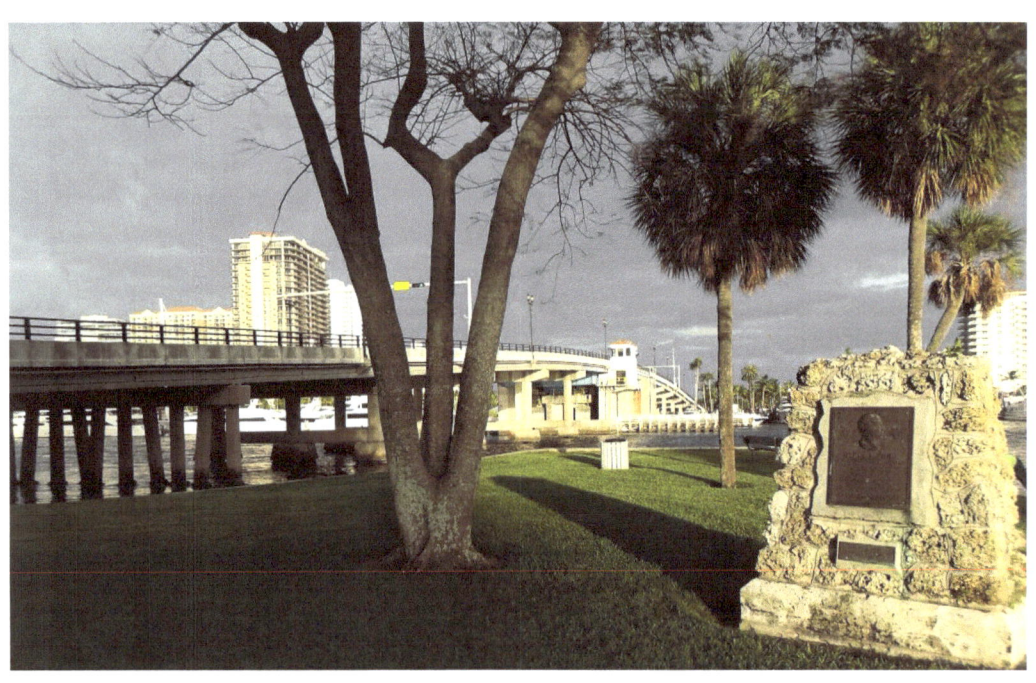

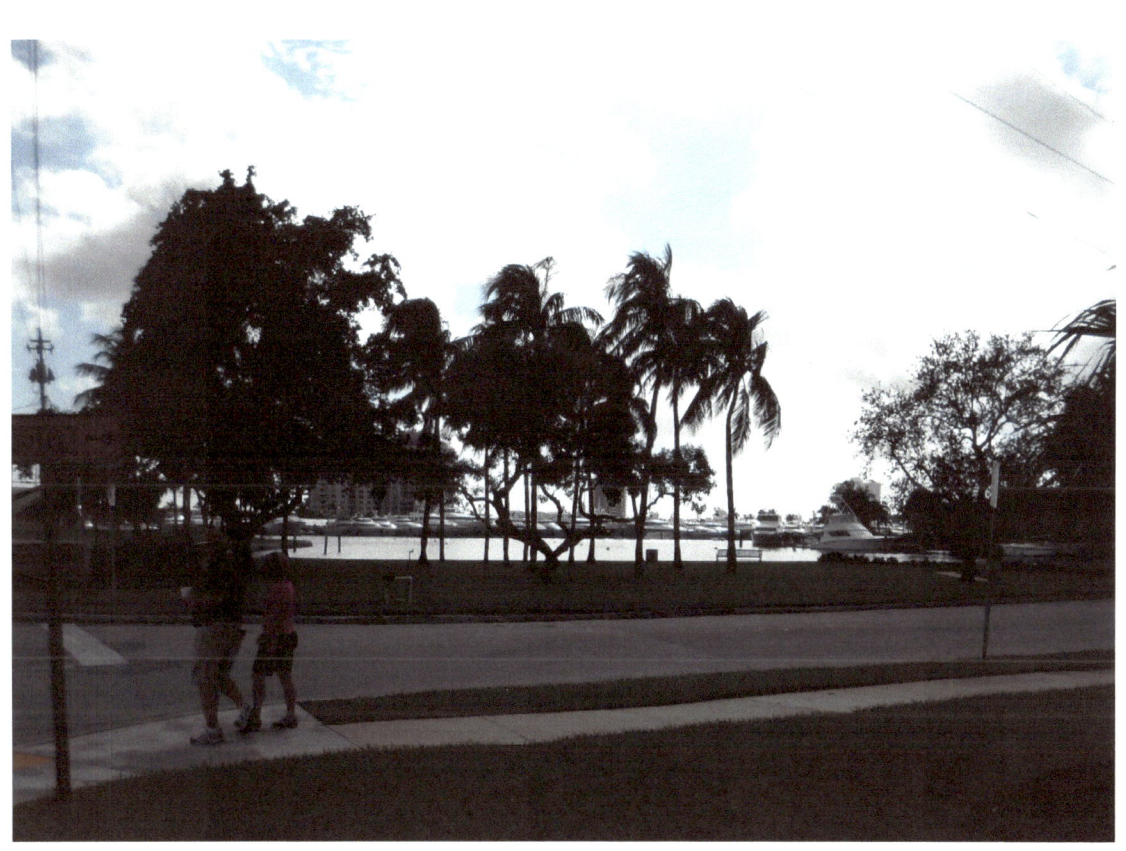

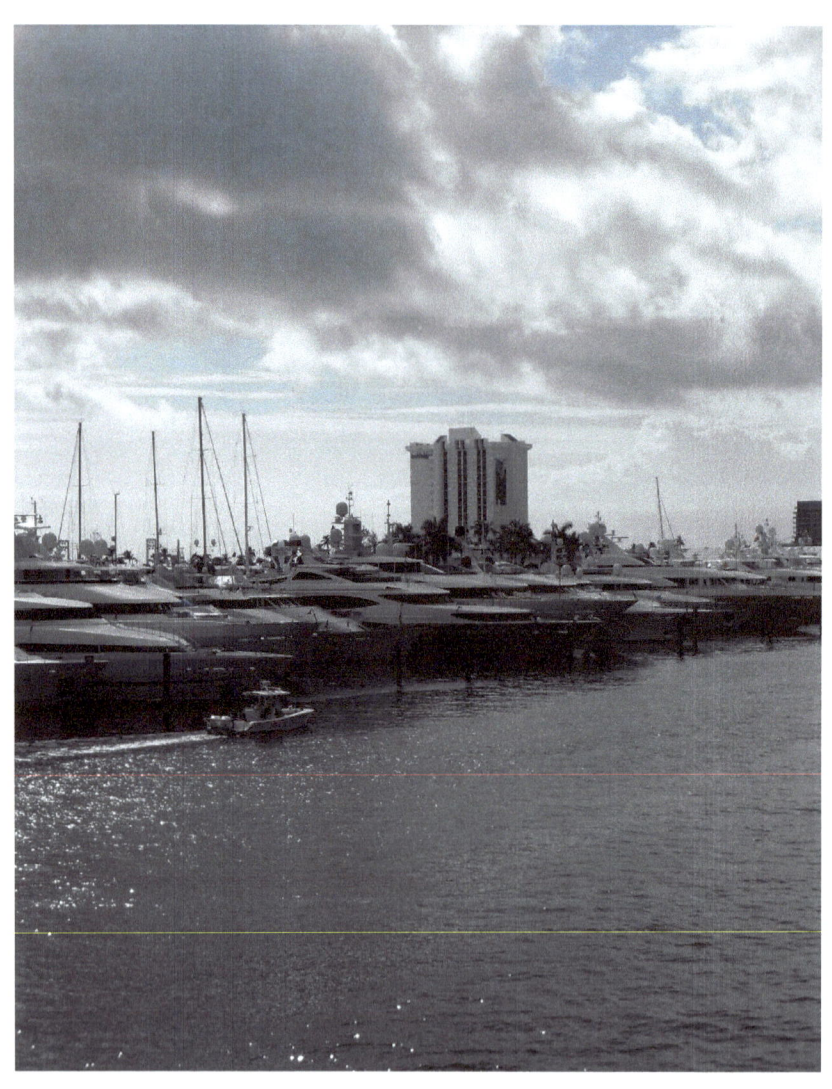

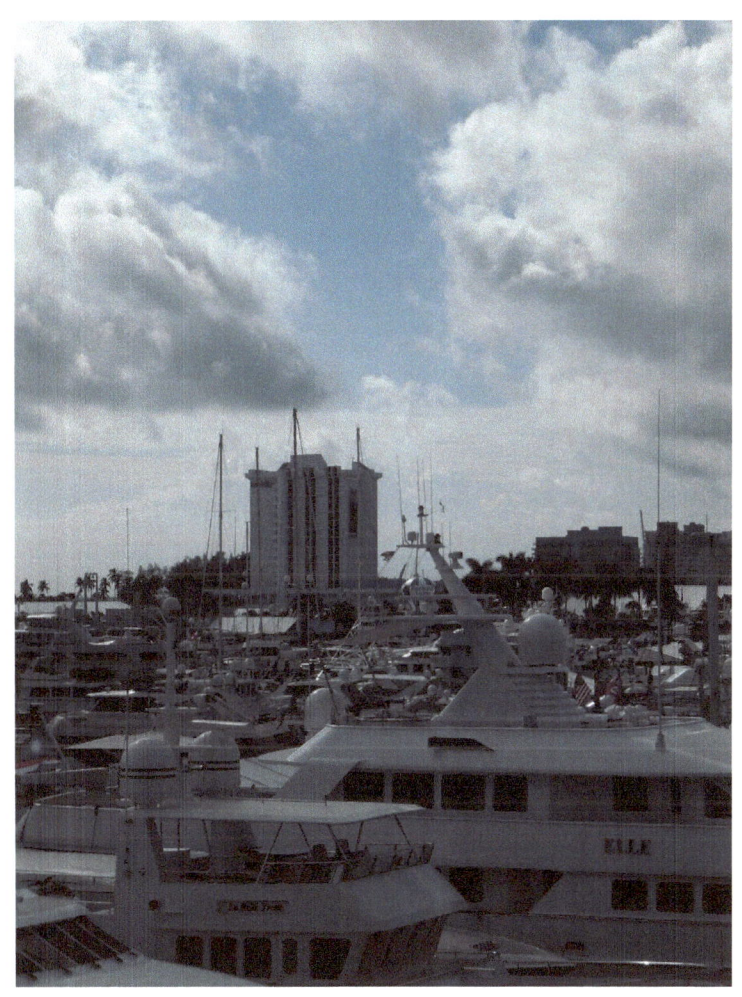

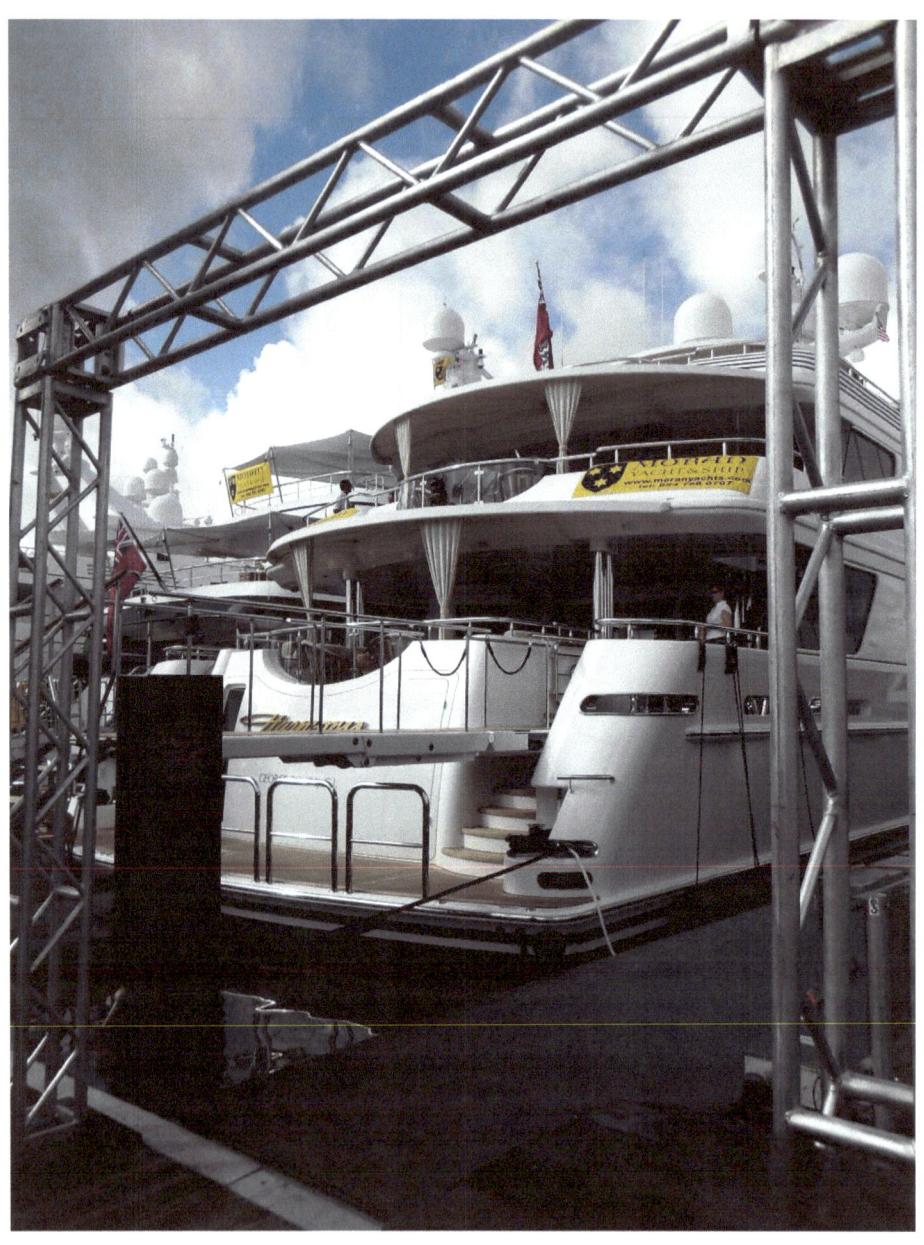

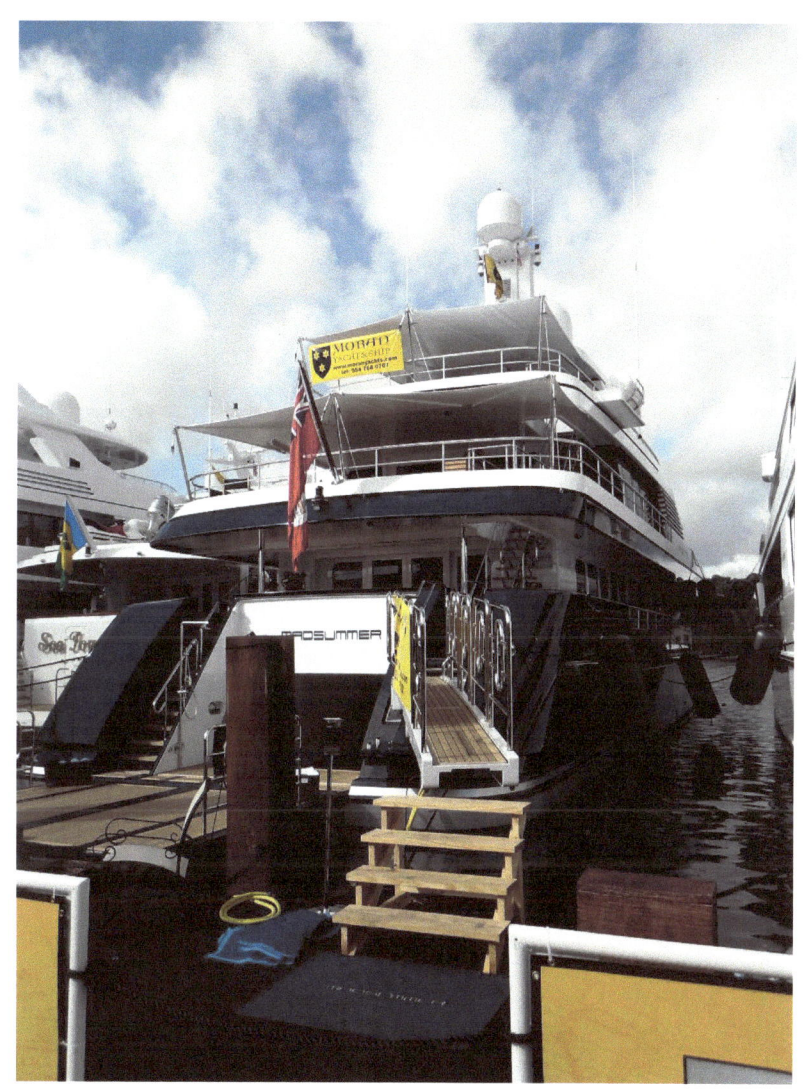

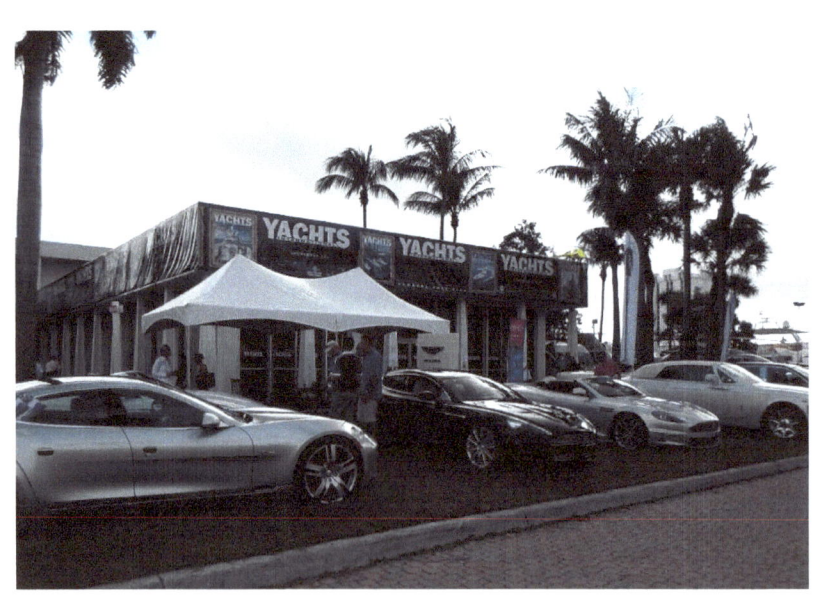

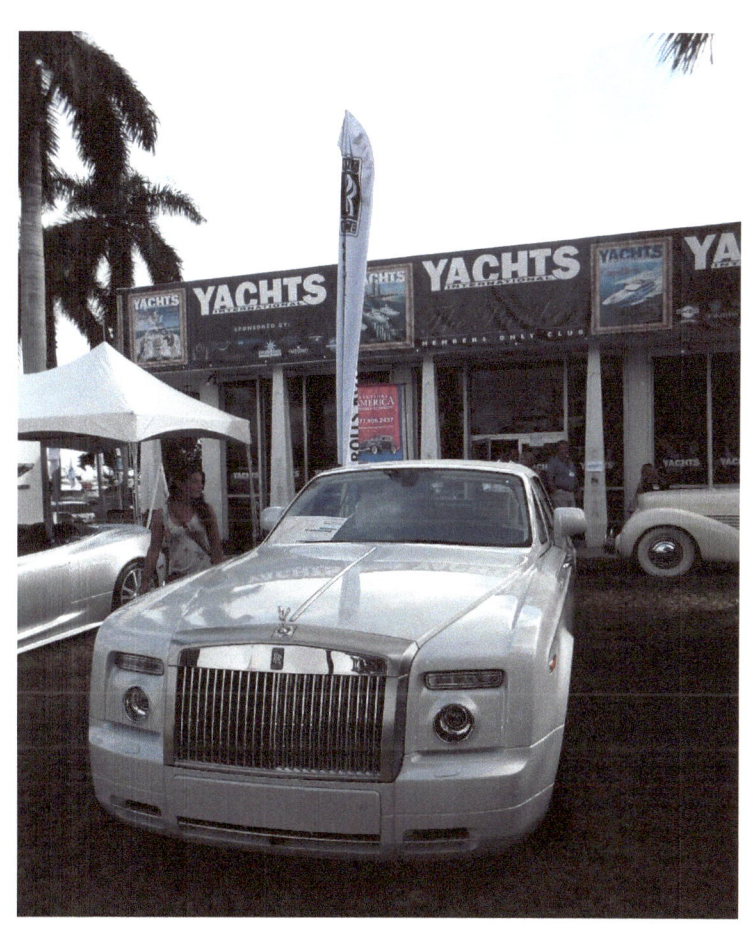

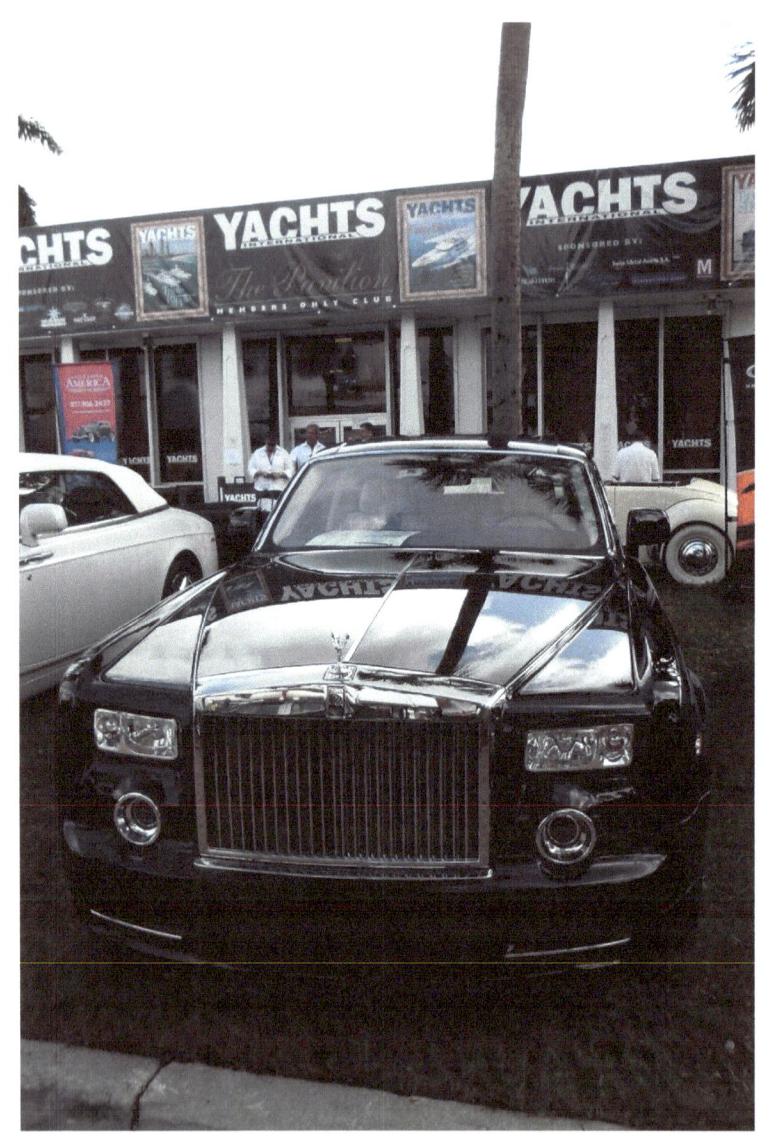

48

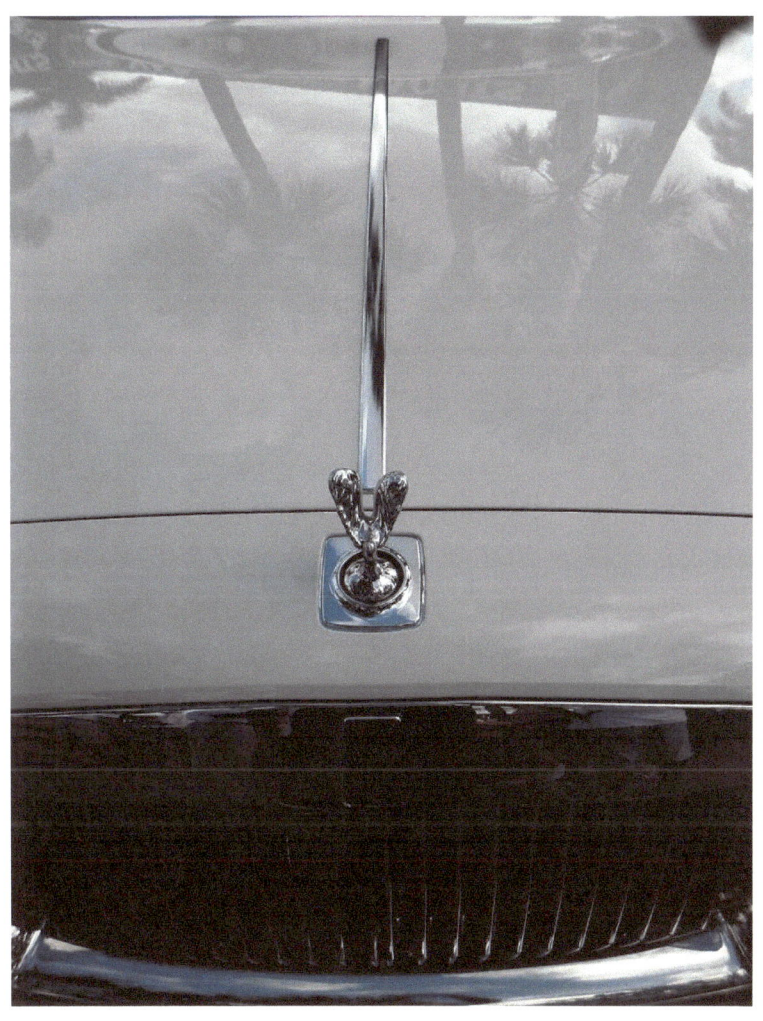

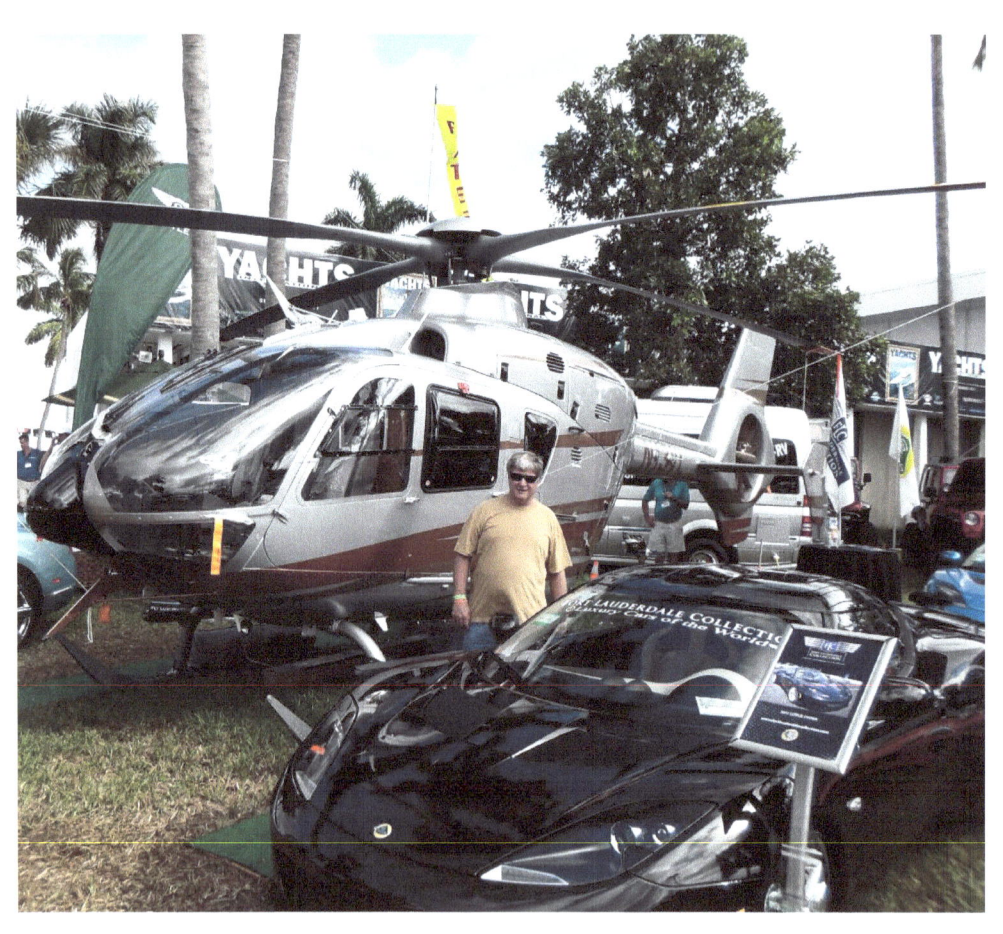

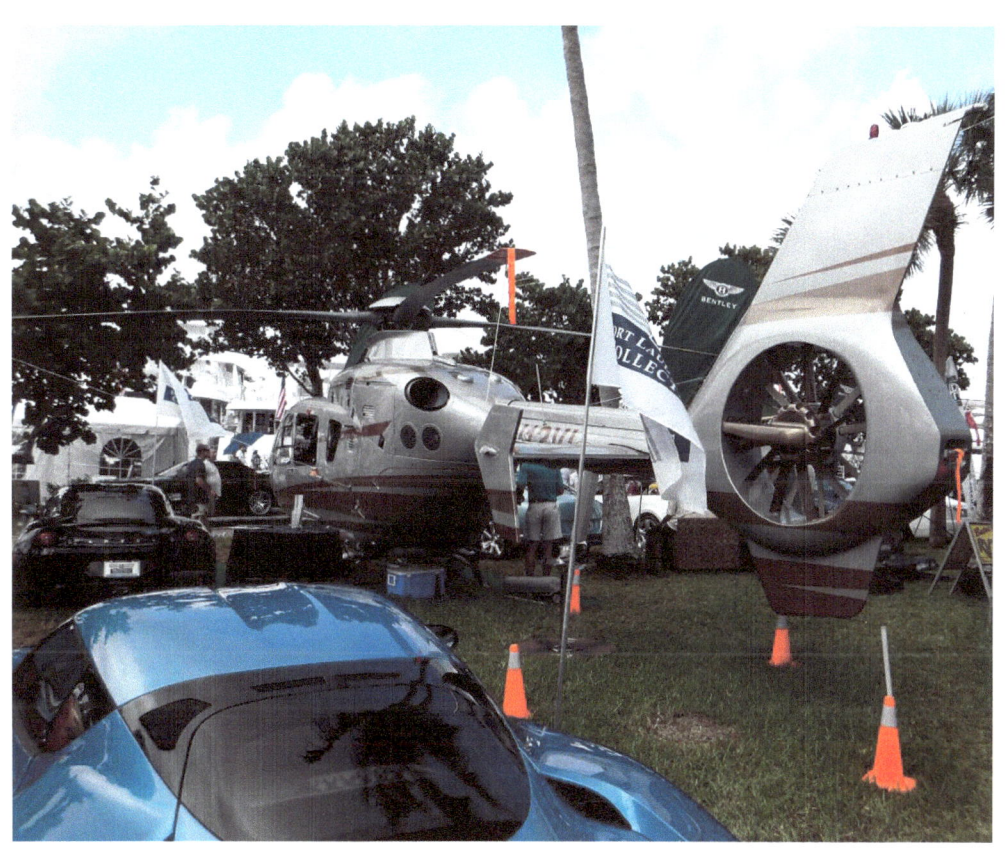

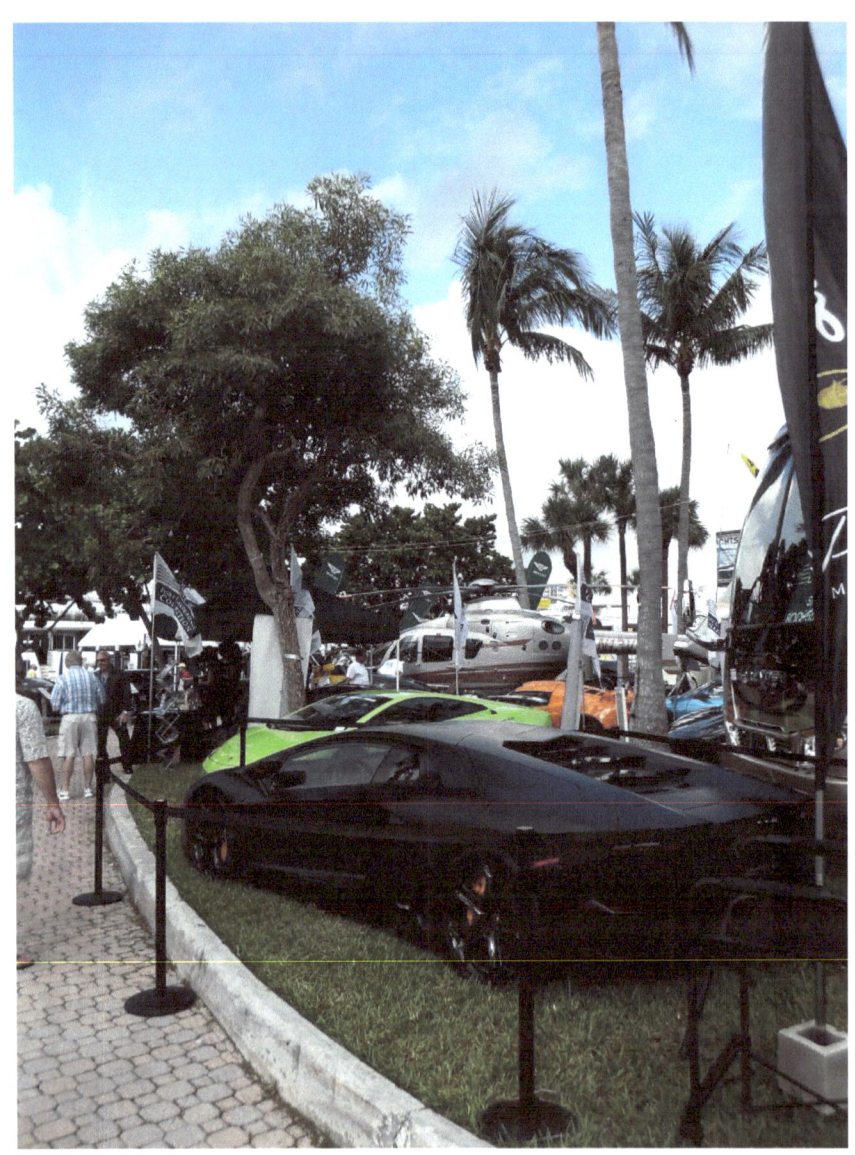

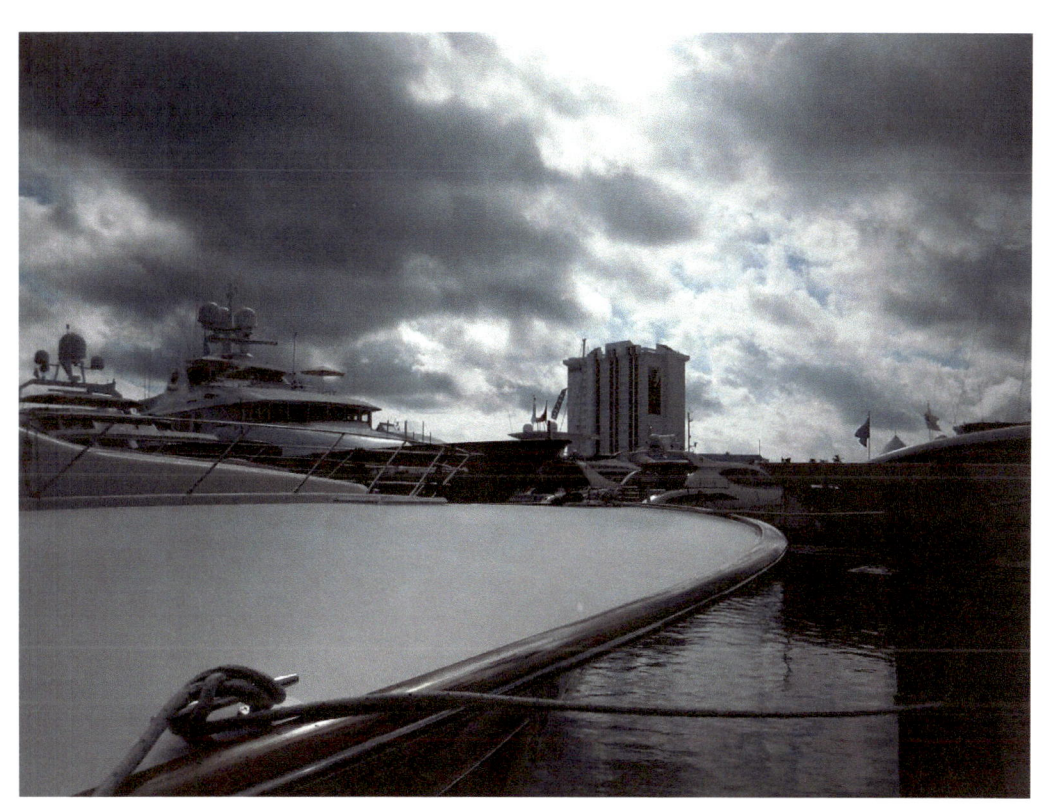

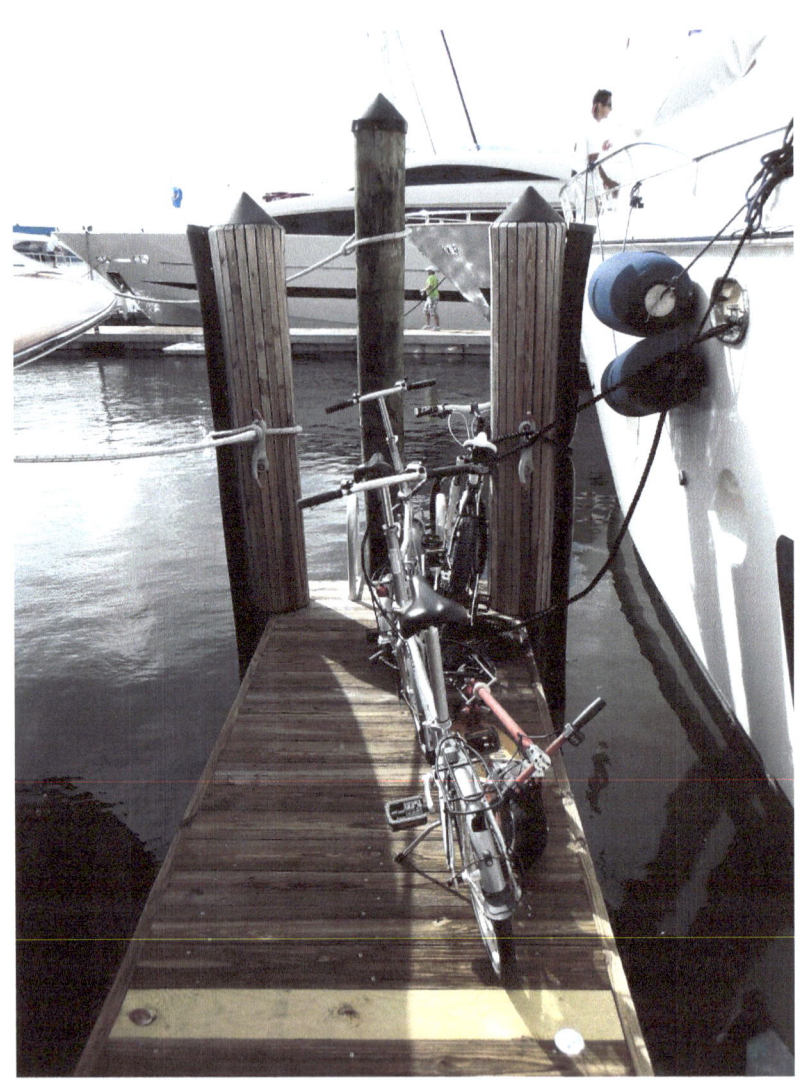

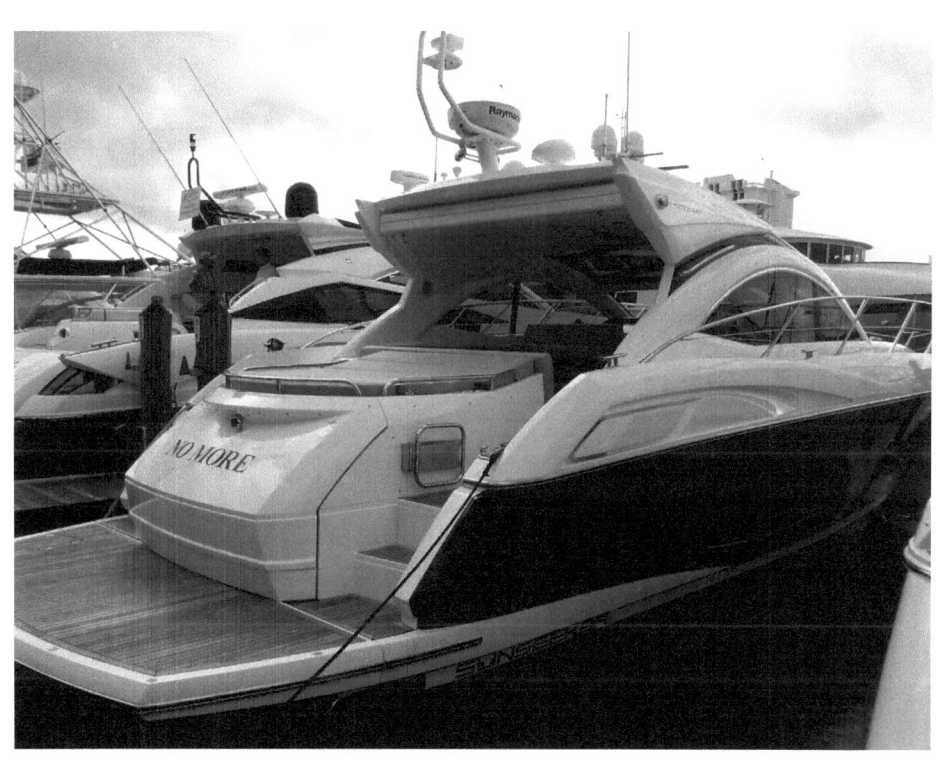

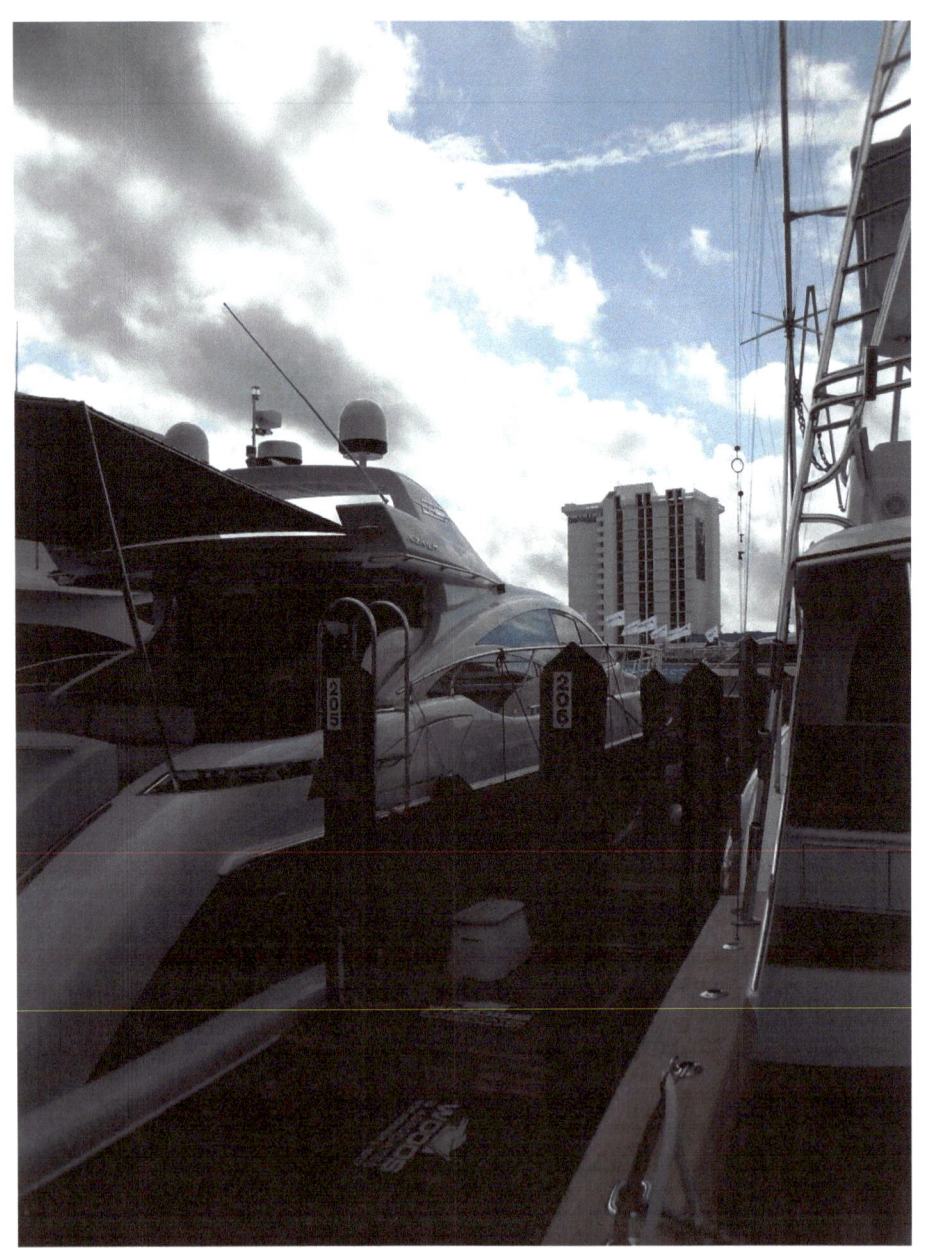

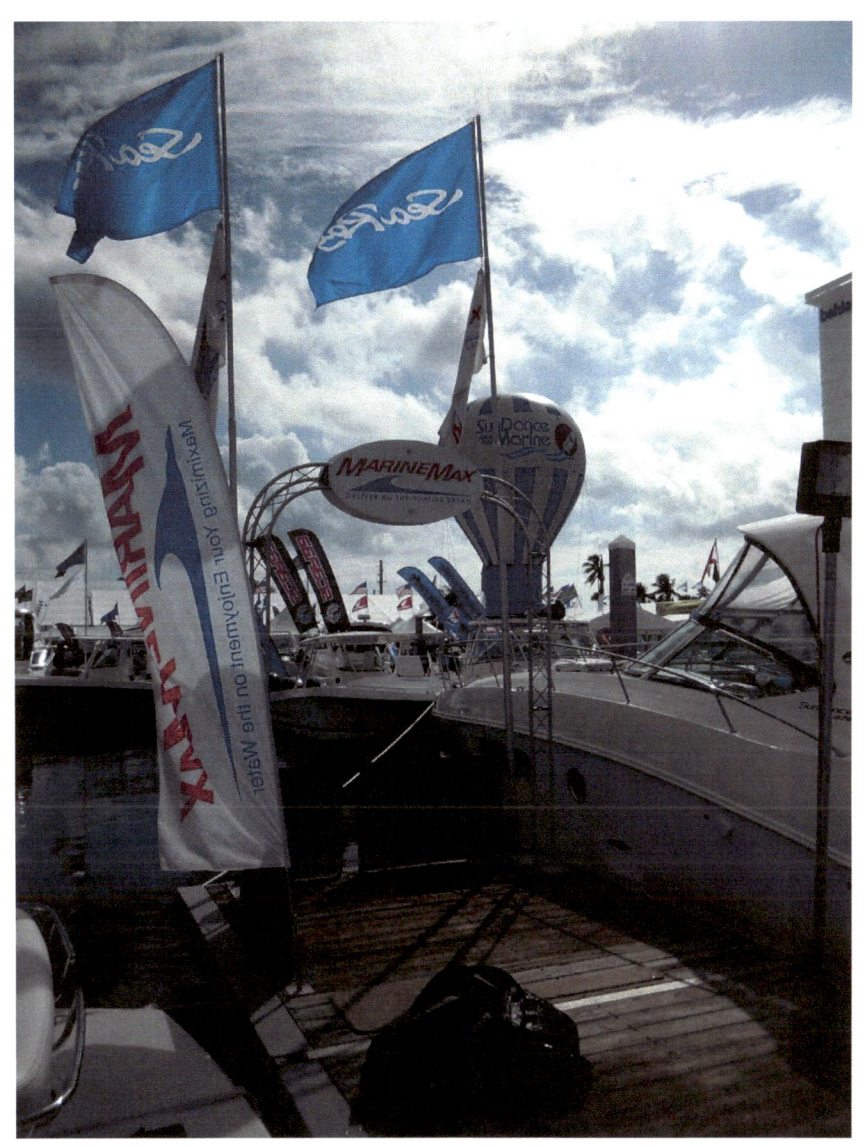

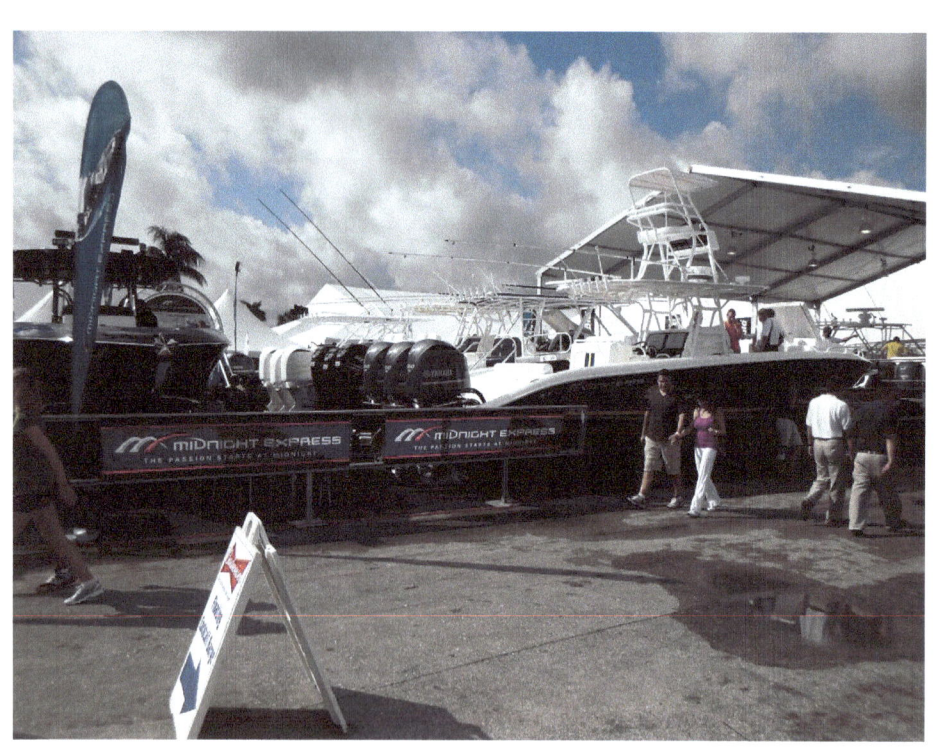

Yachting capital

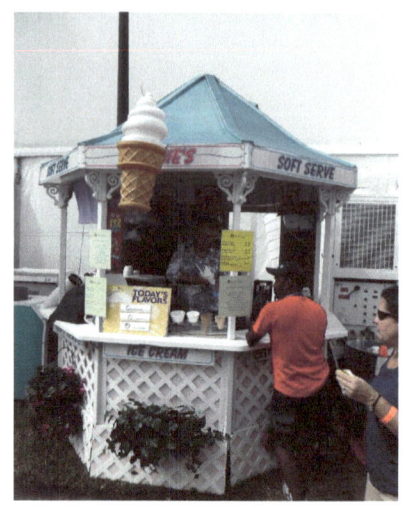

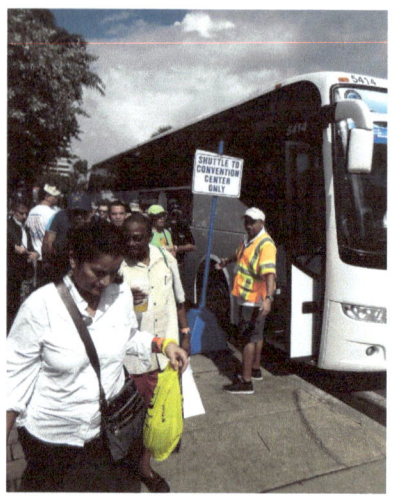

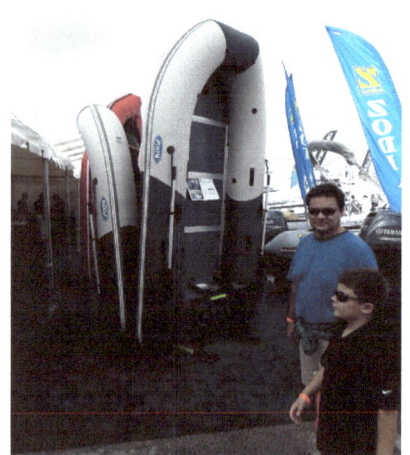

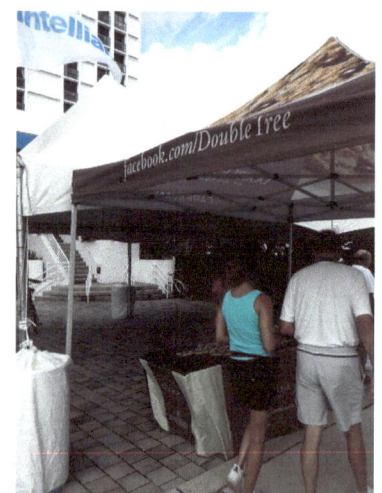

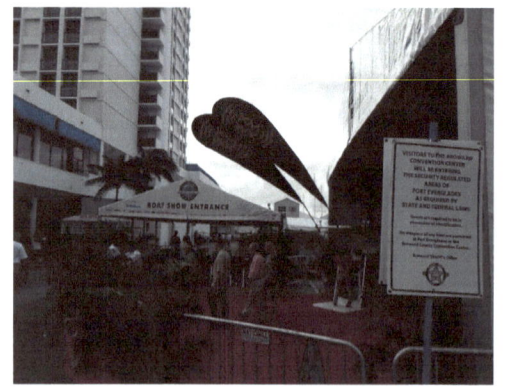

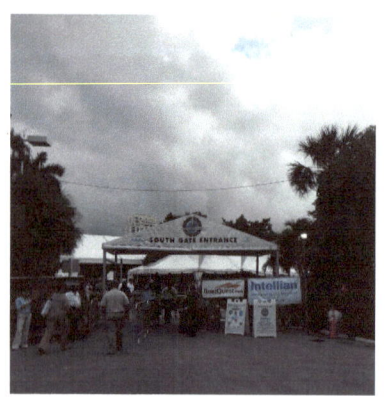

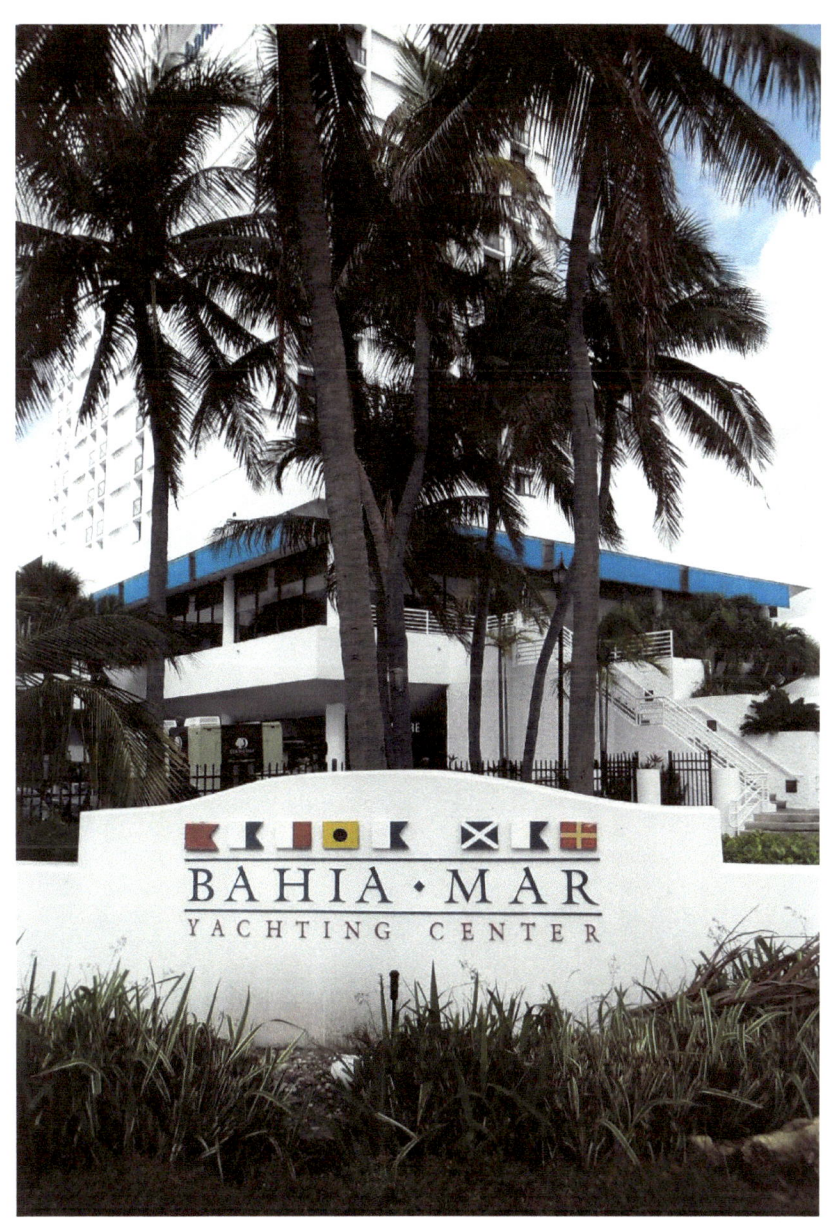

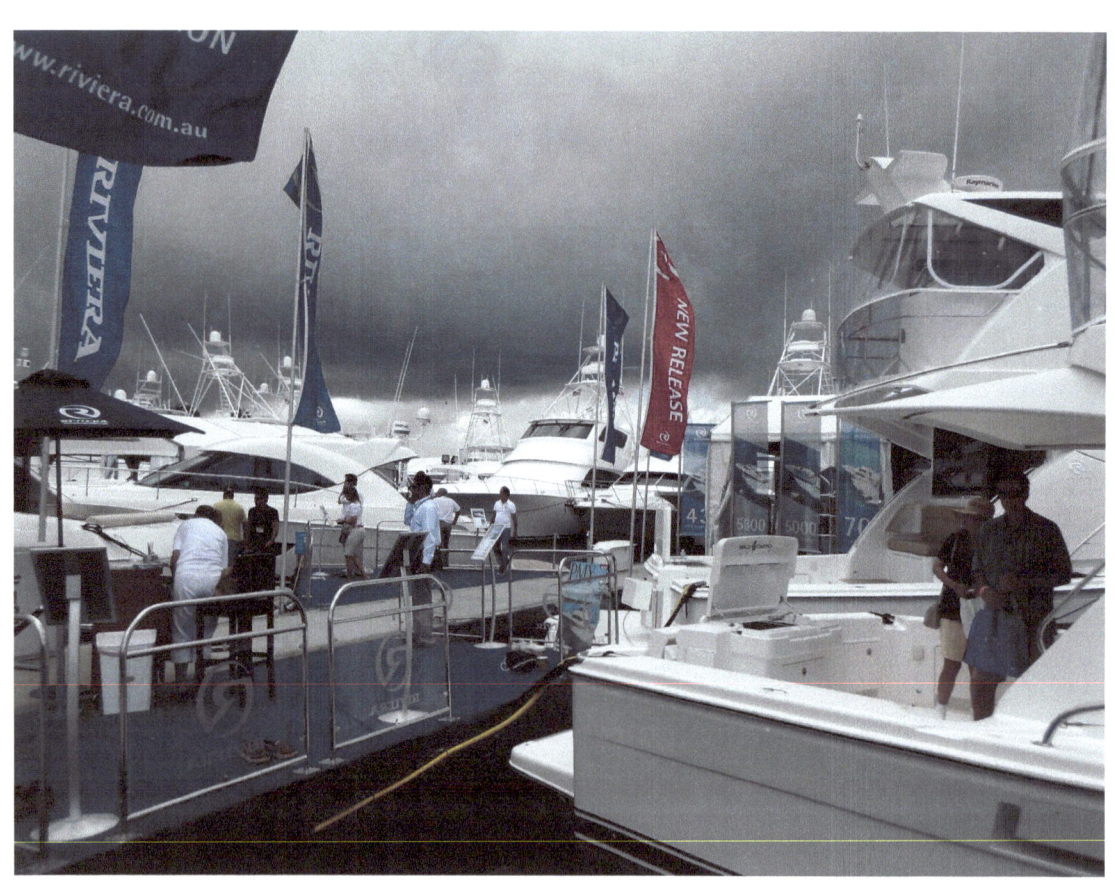

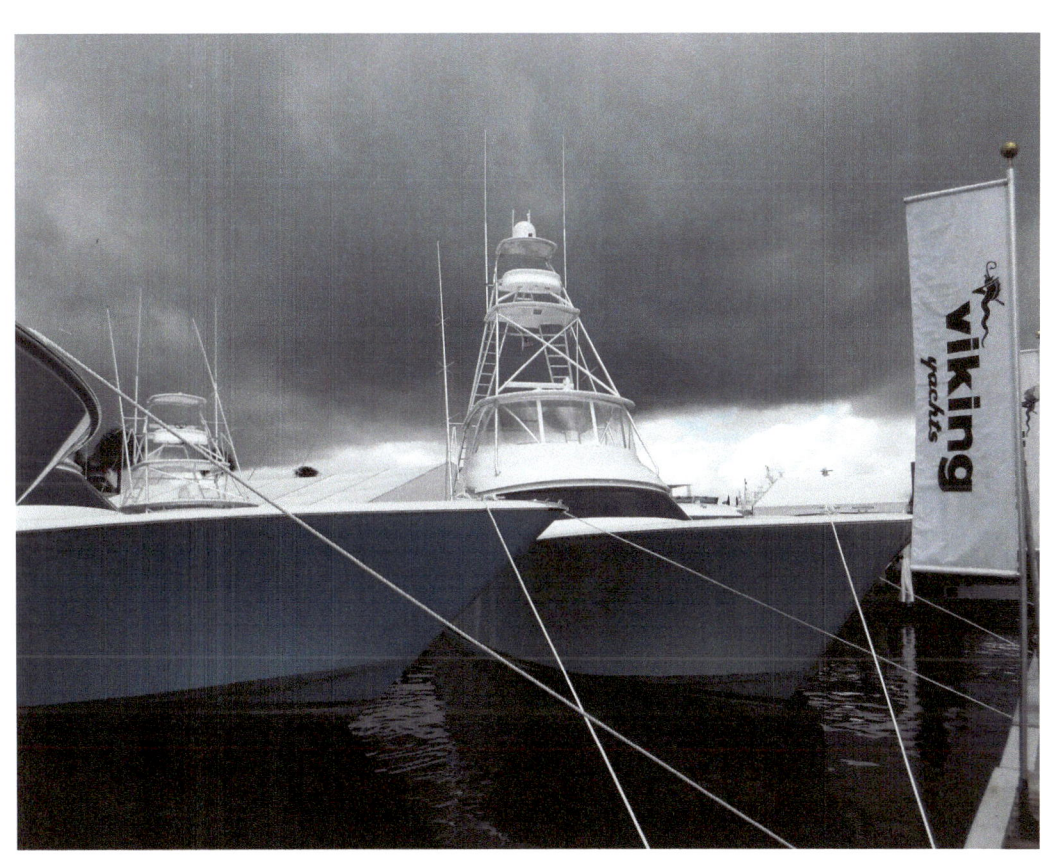

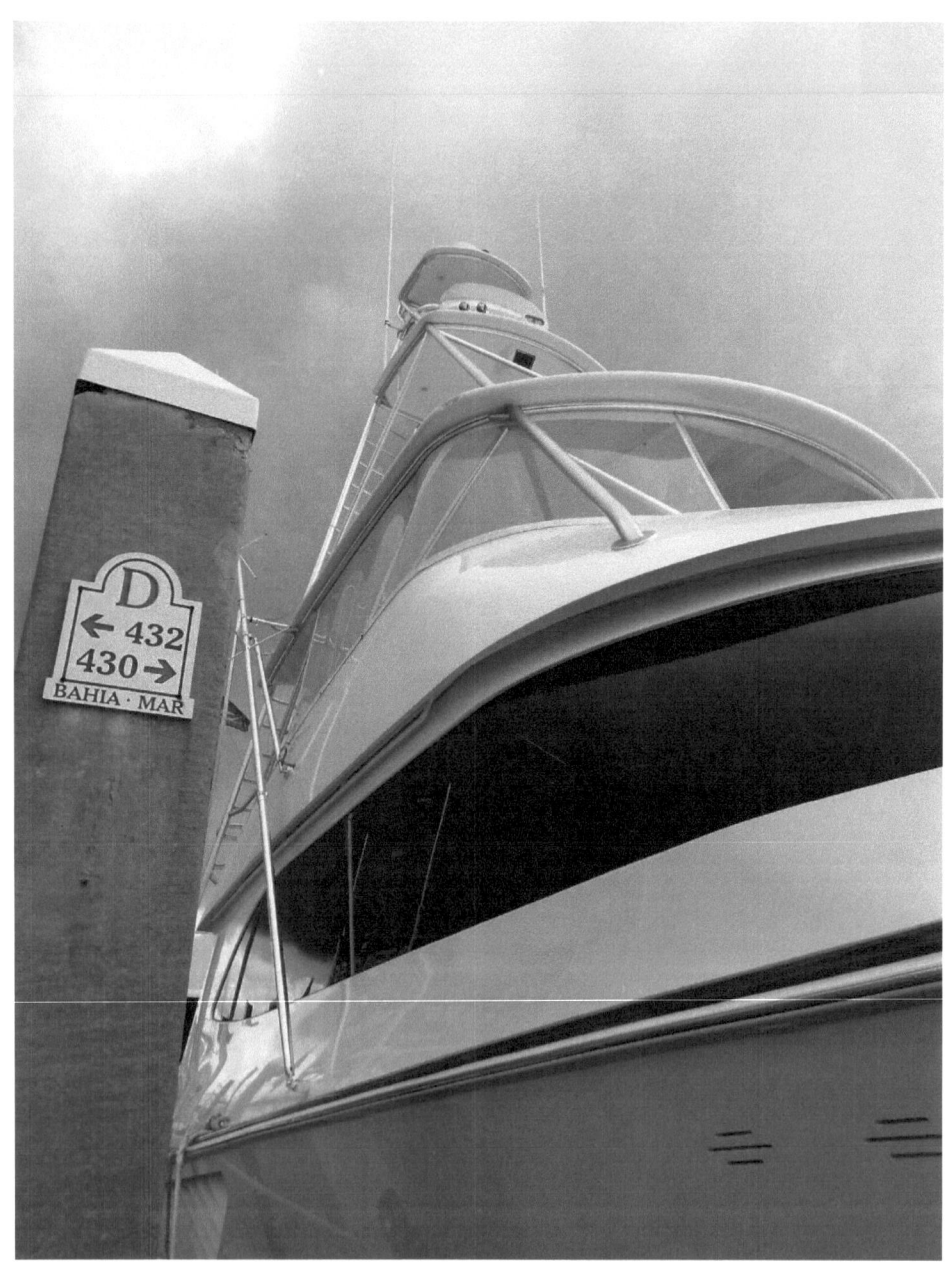

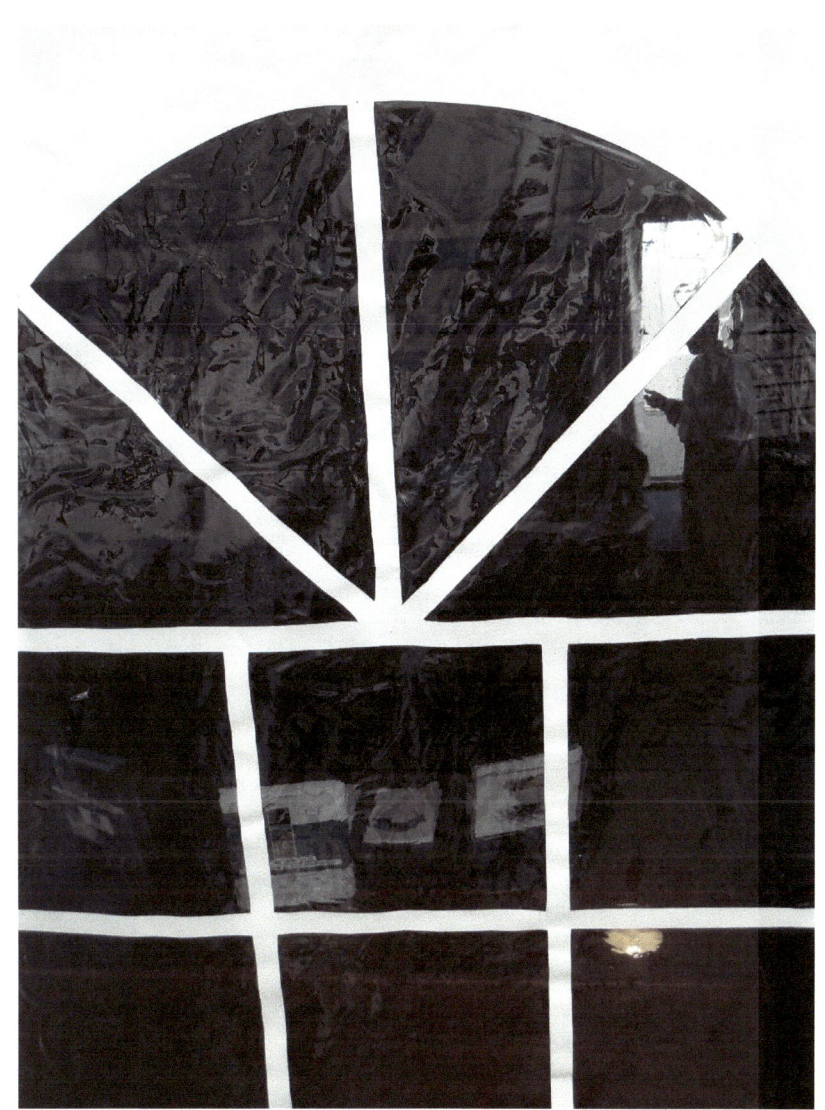

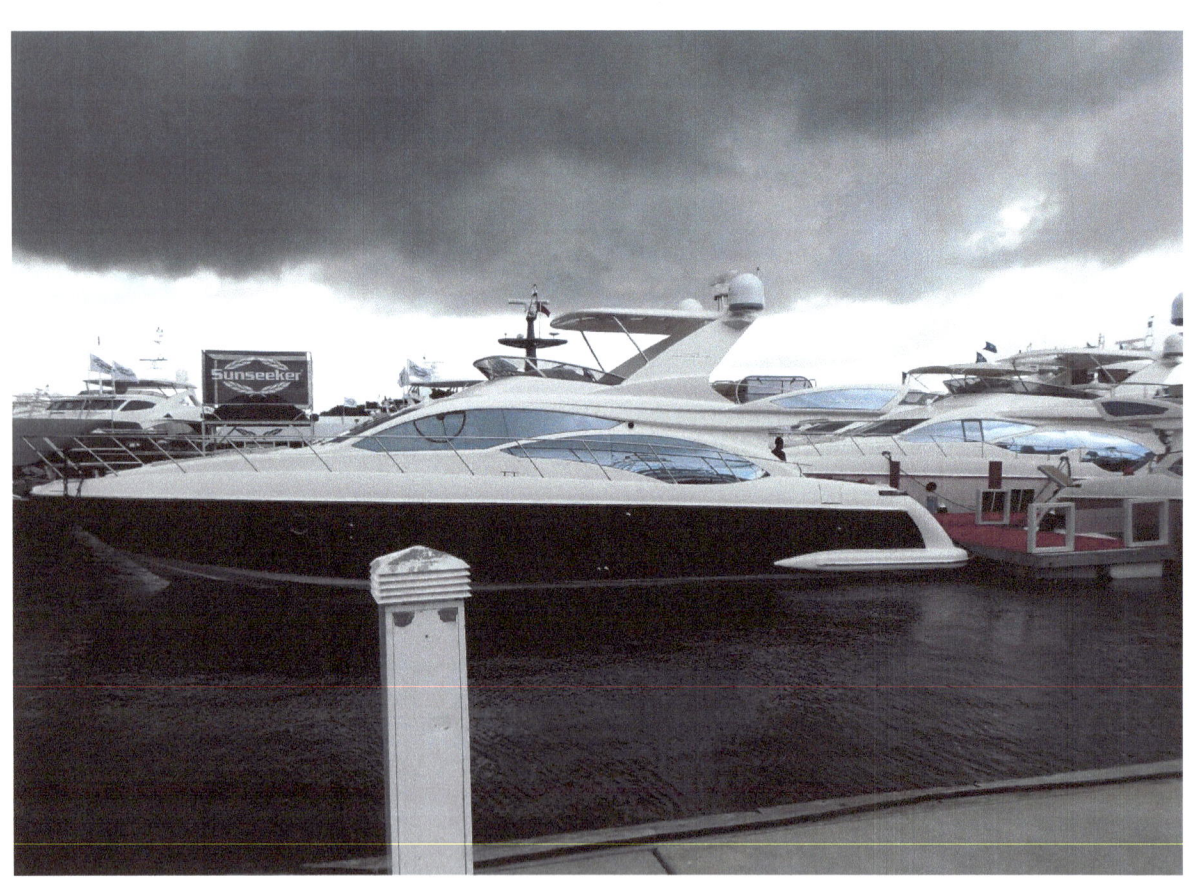

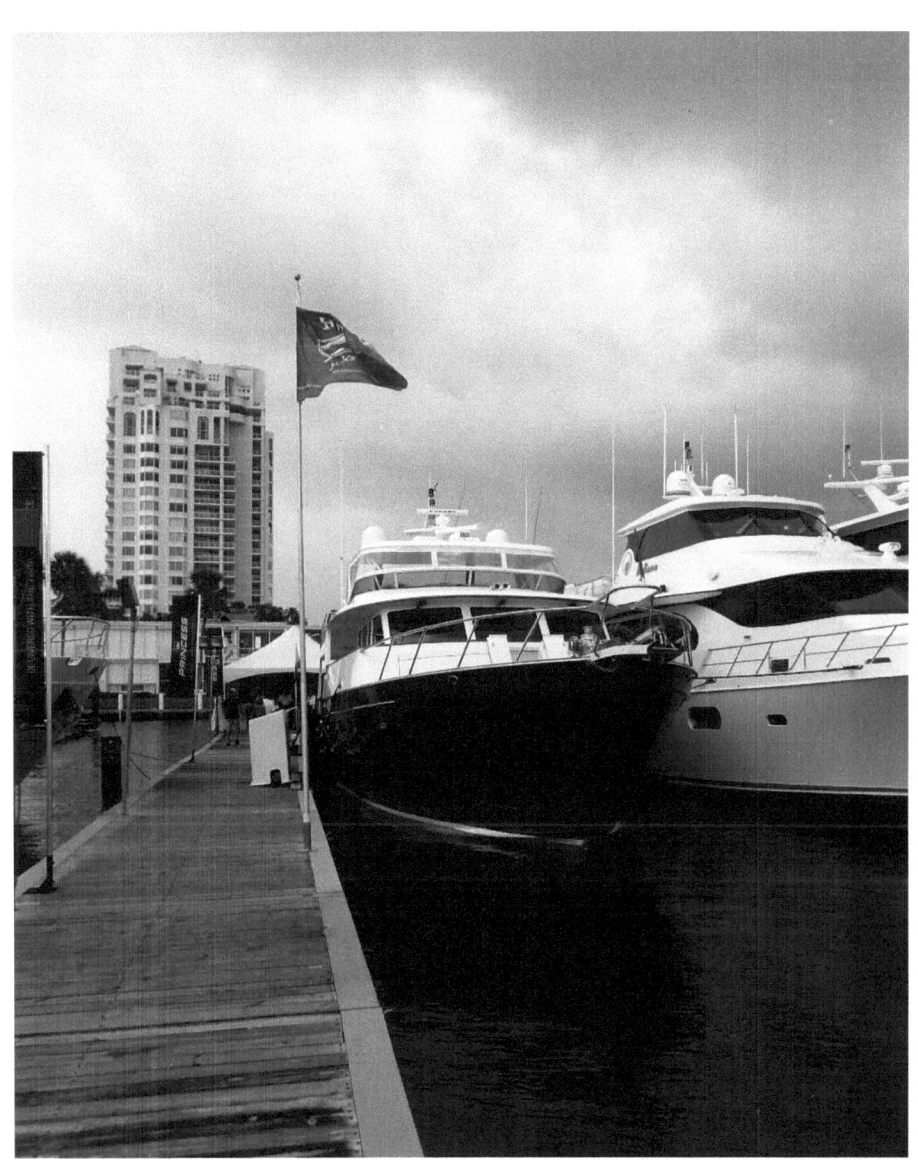

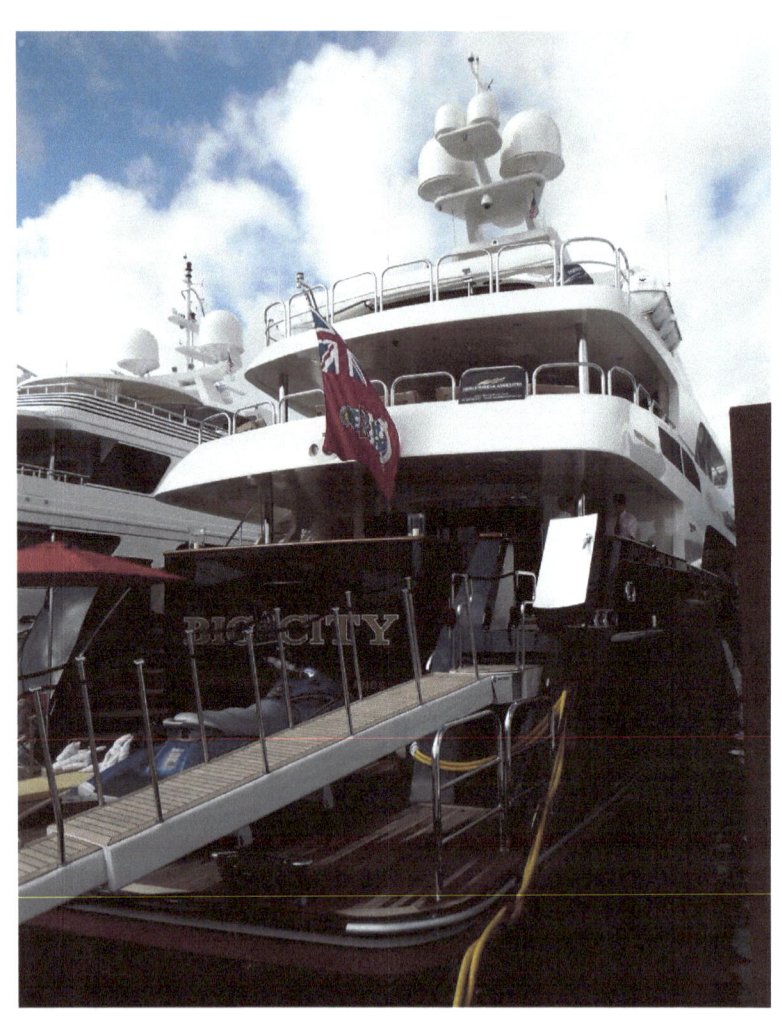

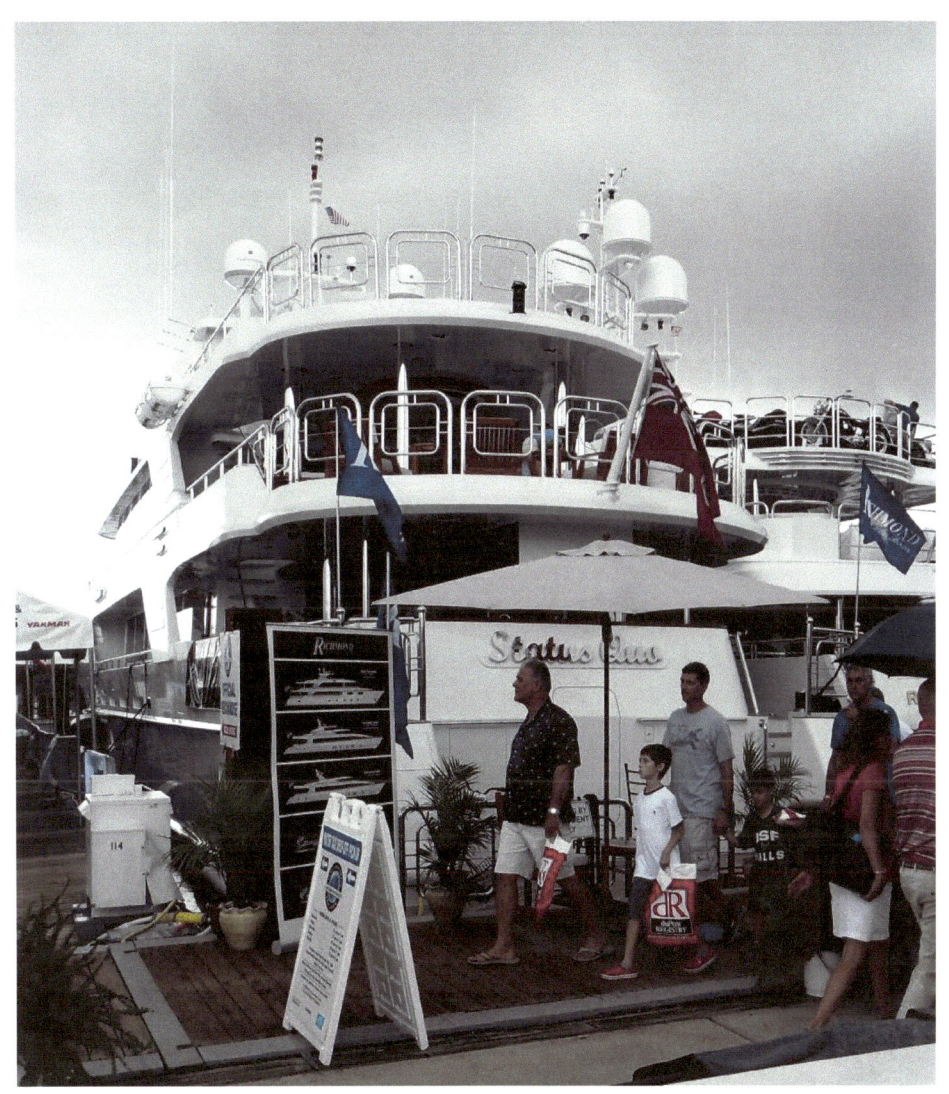

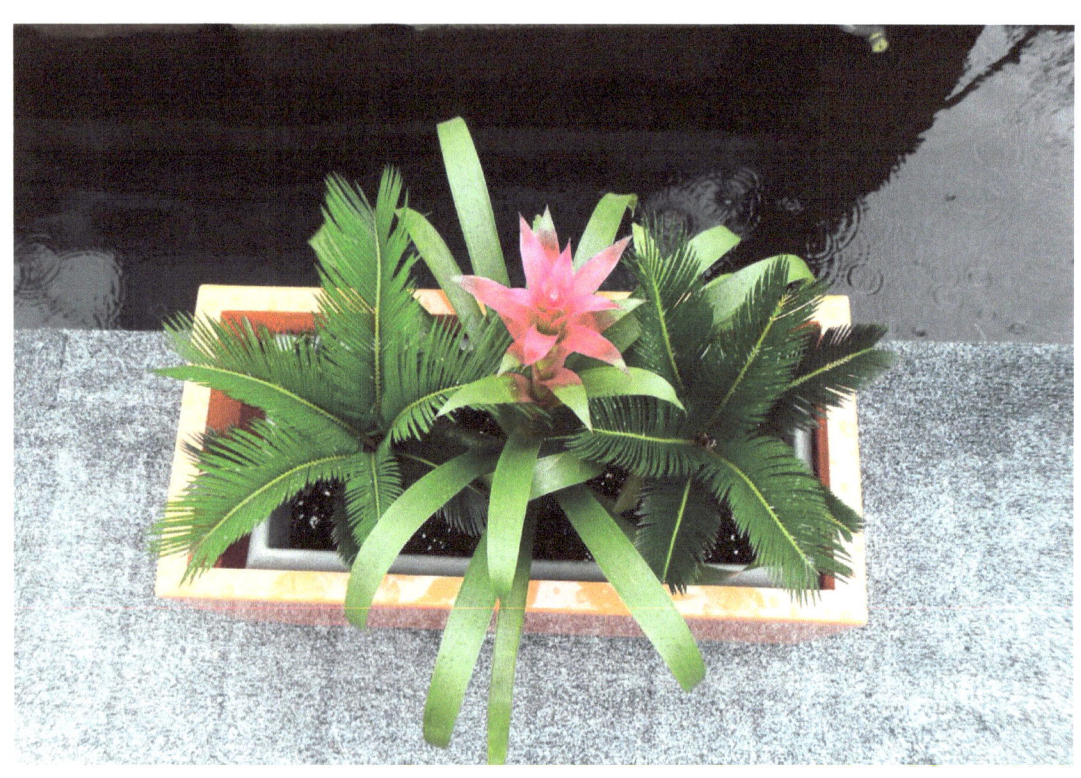

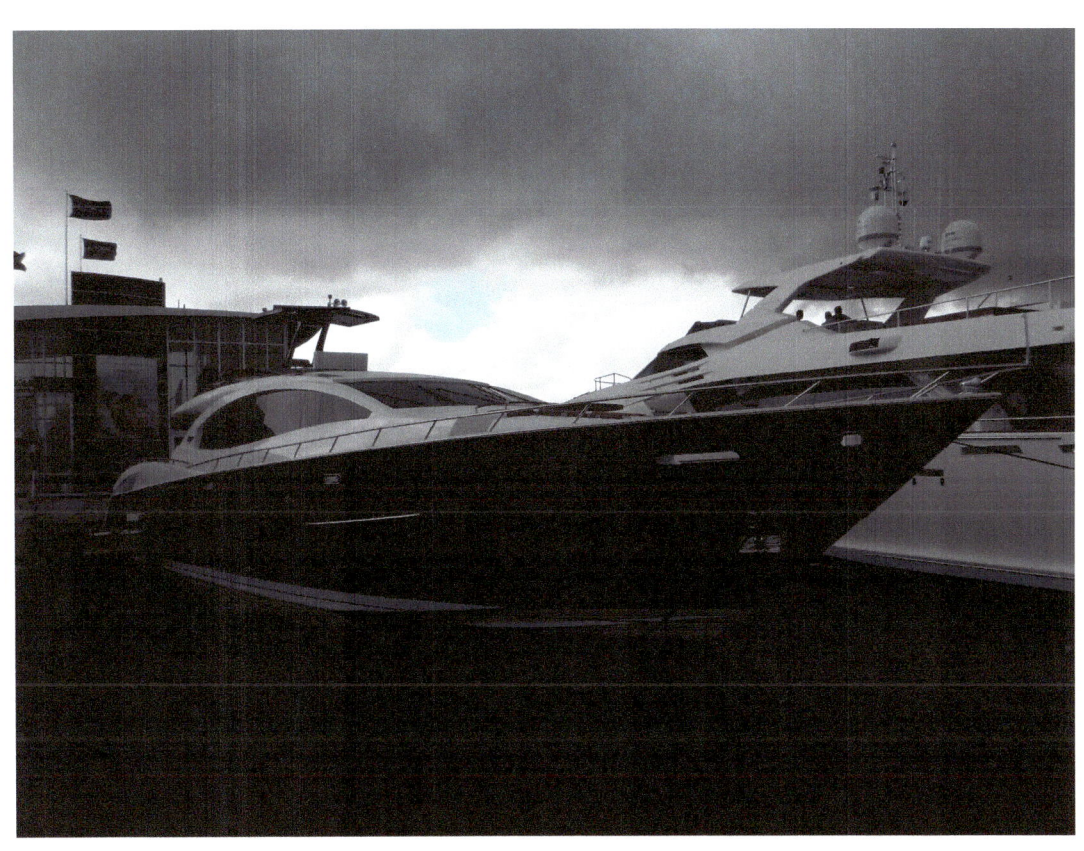

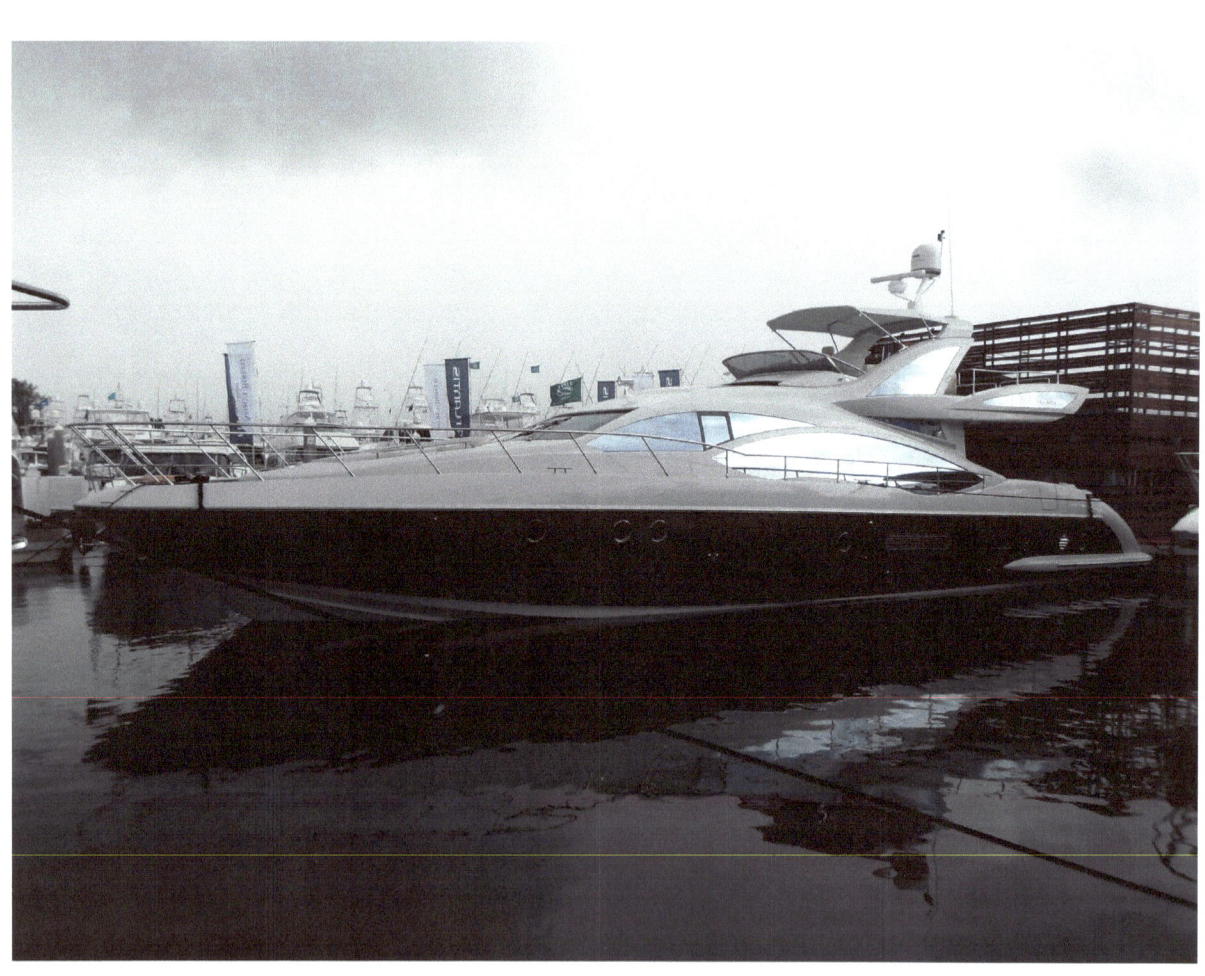

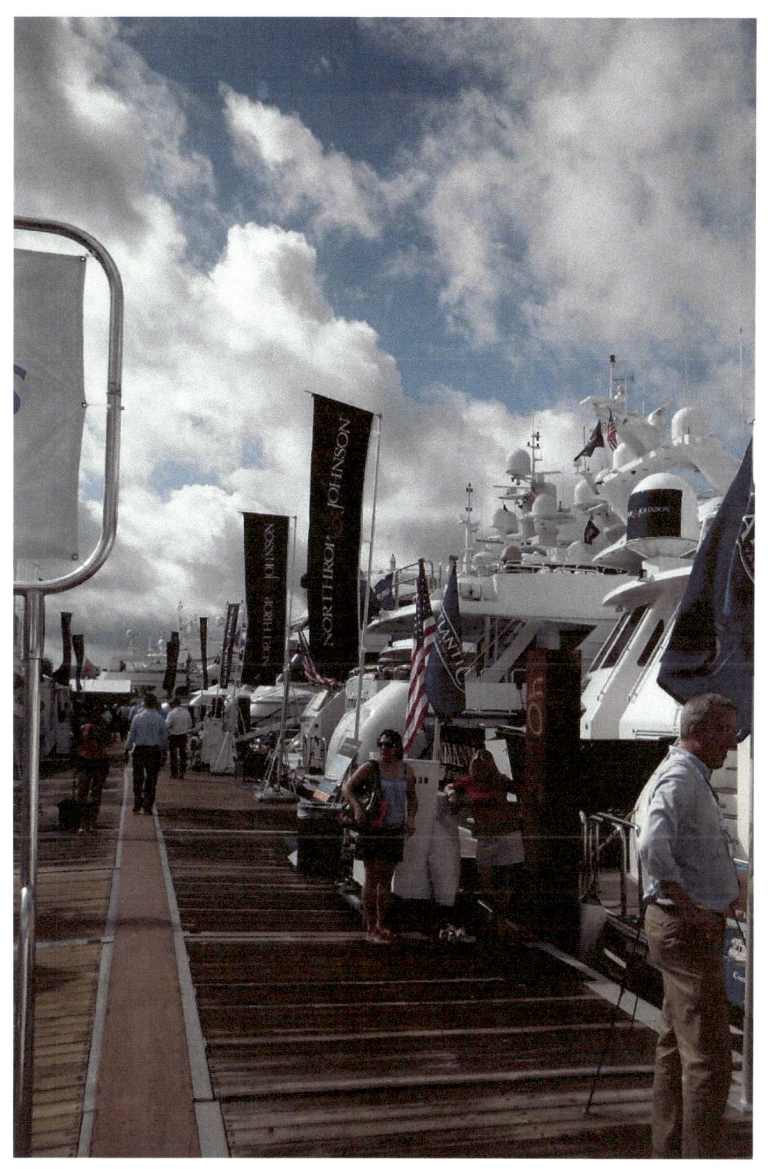

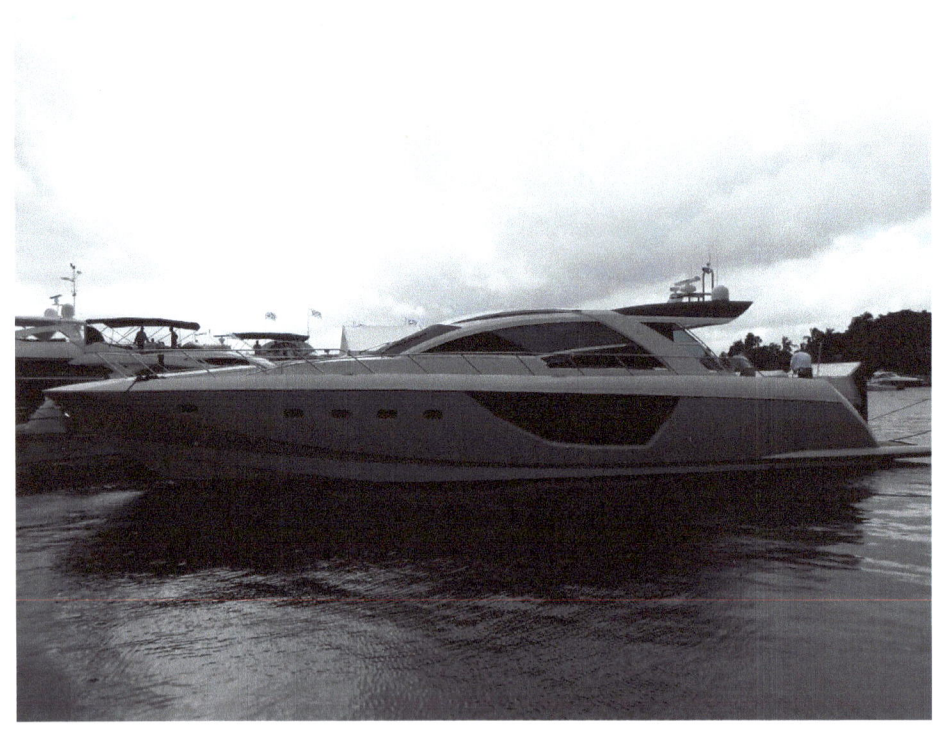

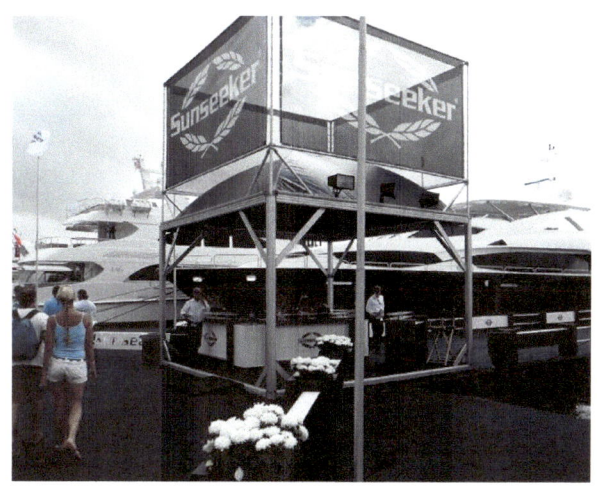
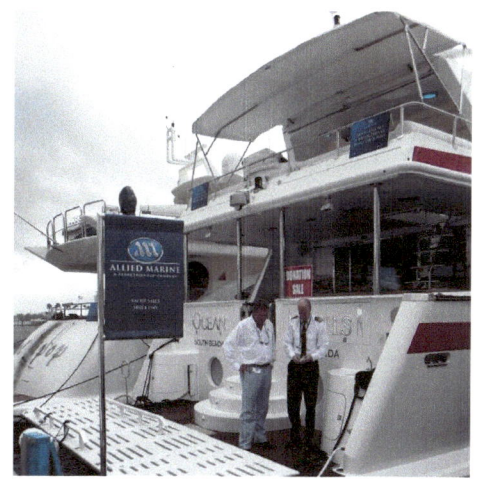
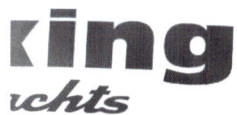
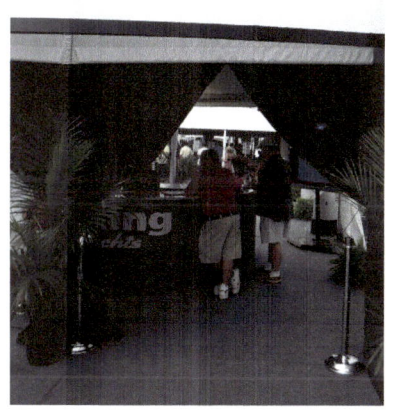
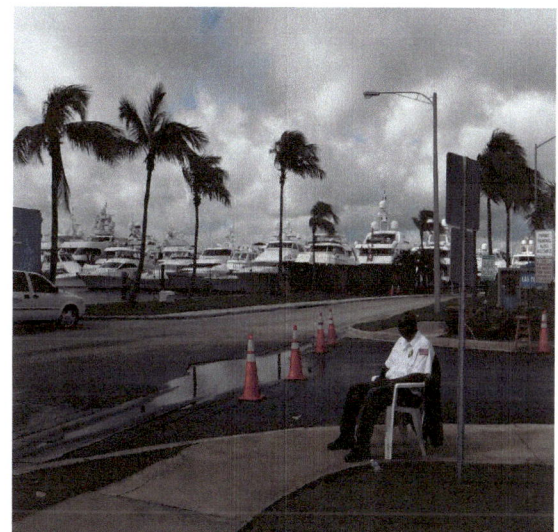
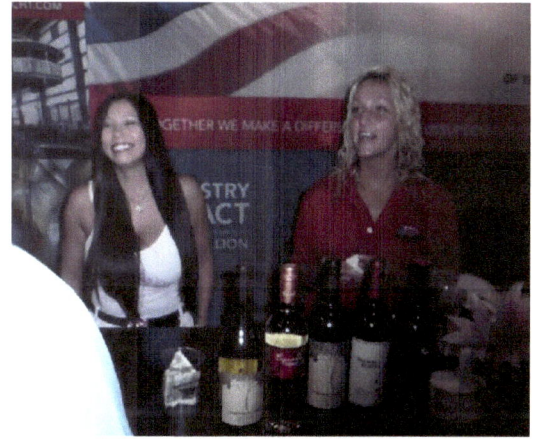
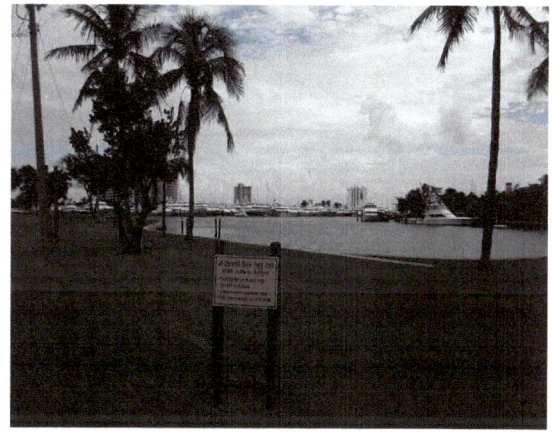

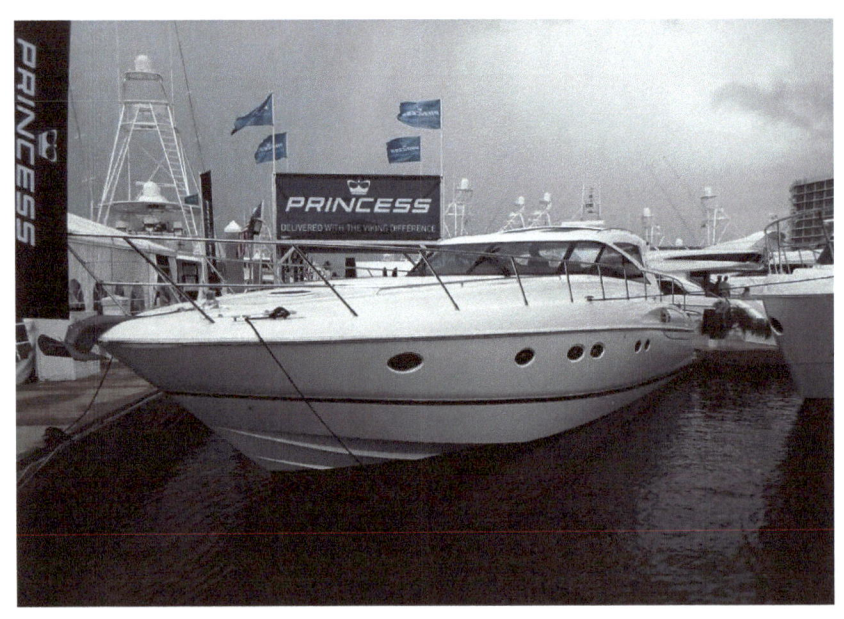

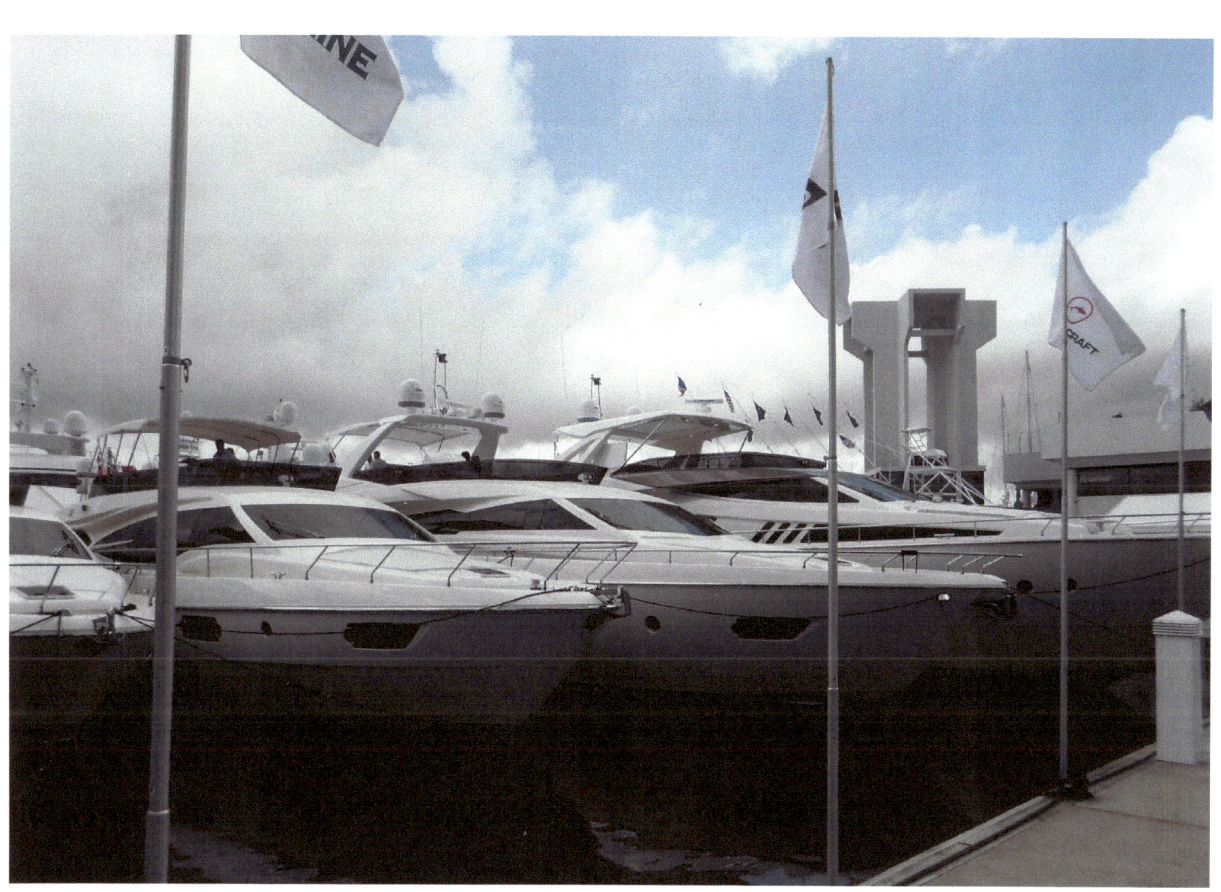

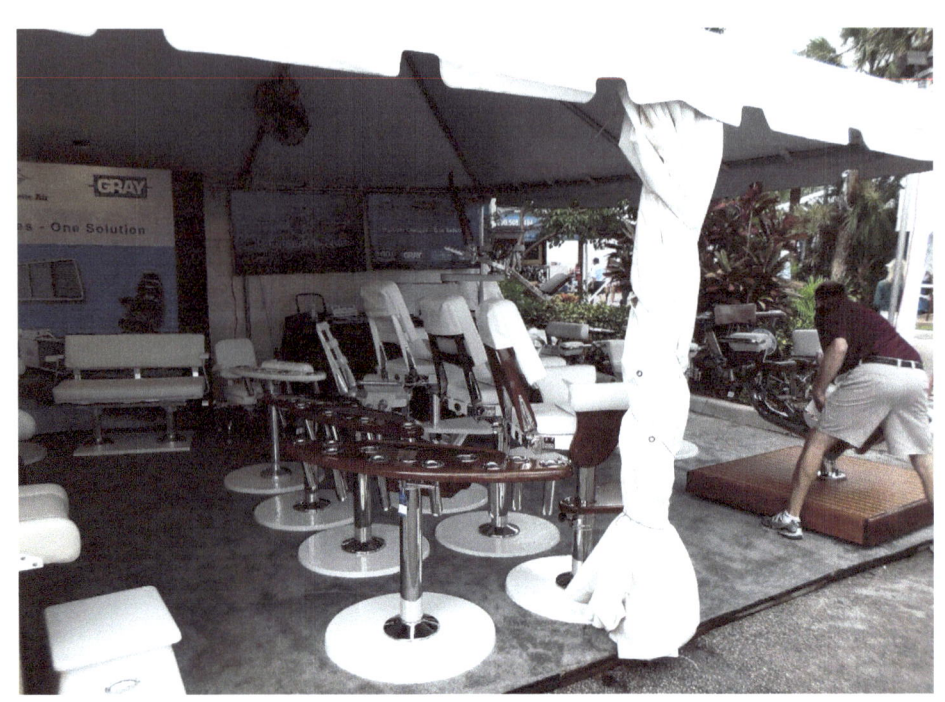

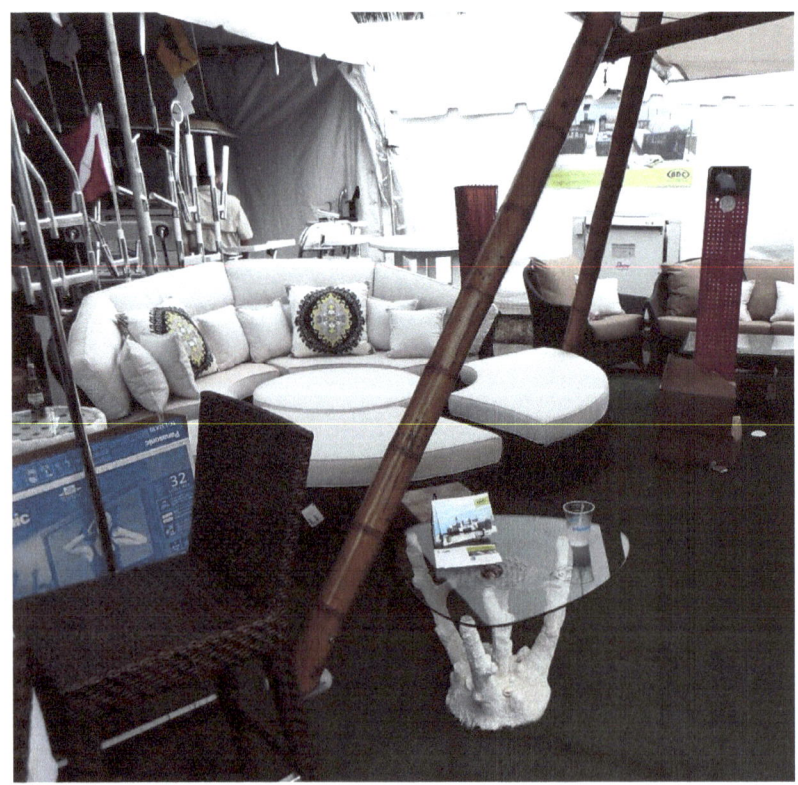

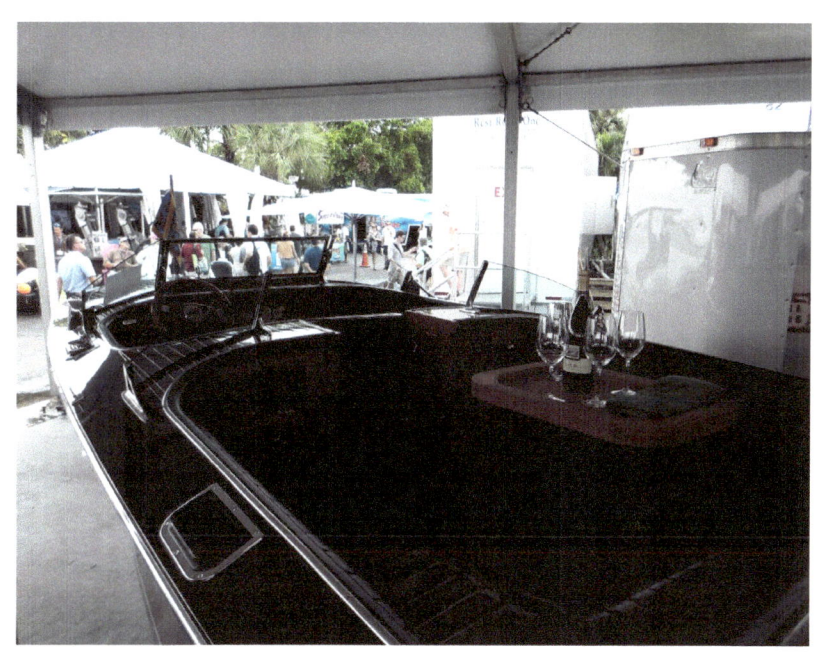

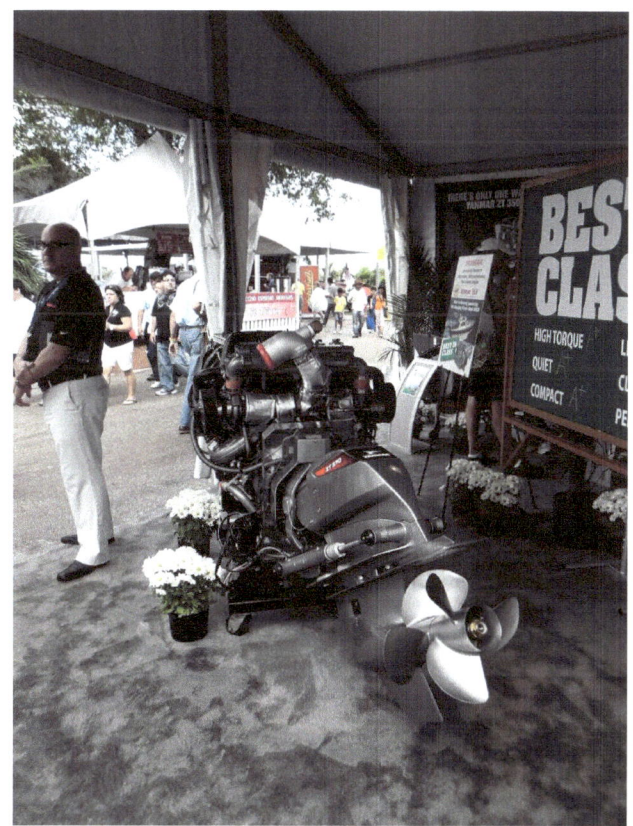

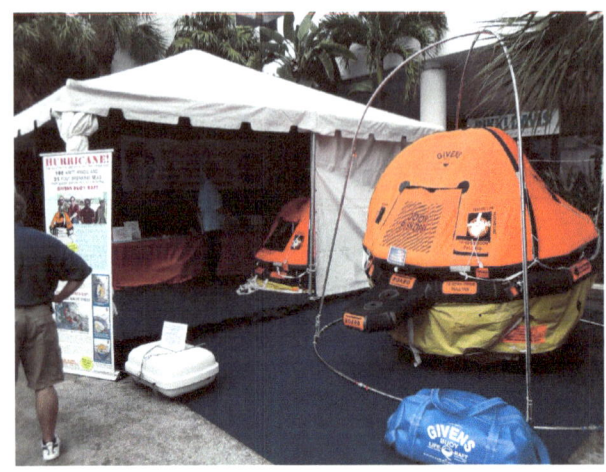

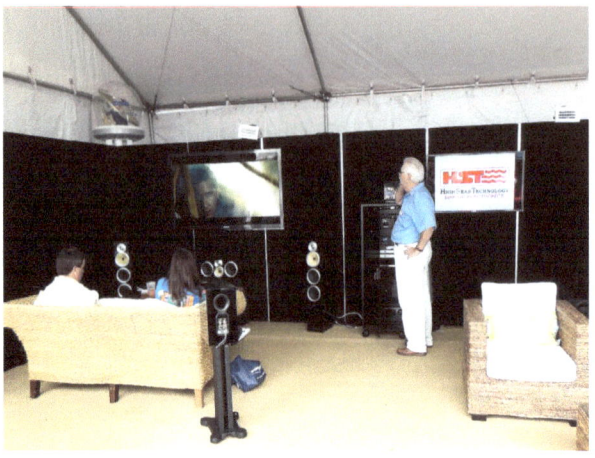

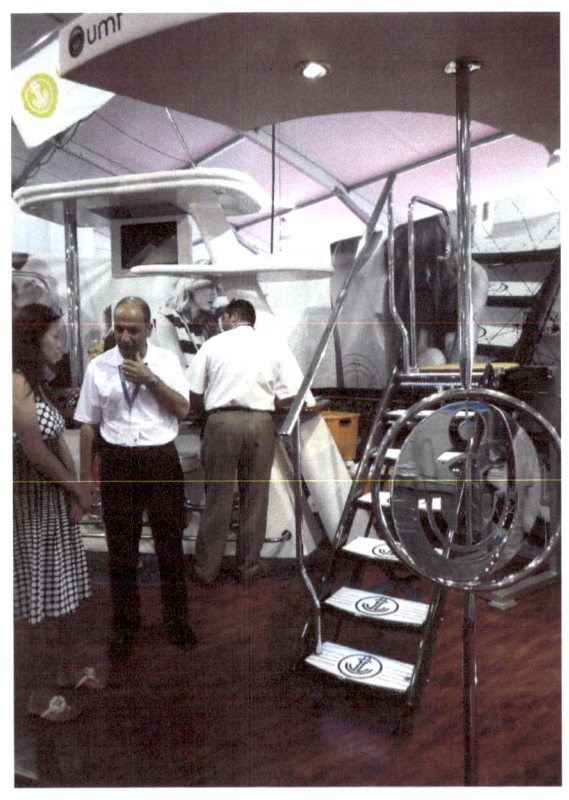

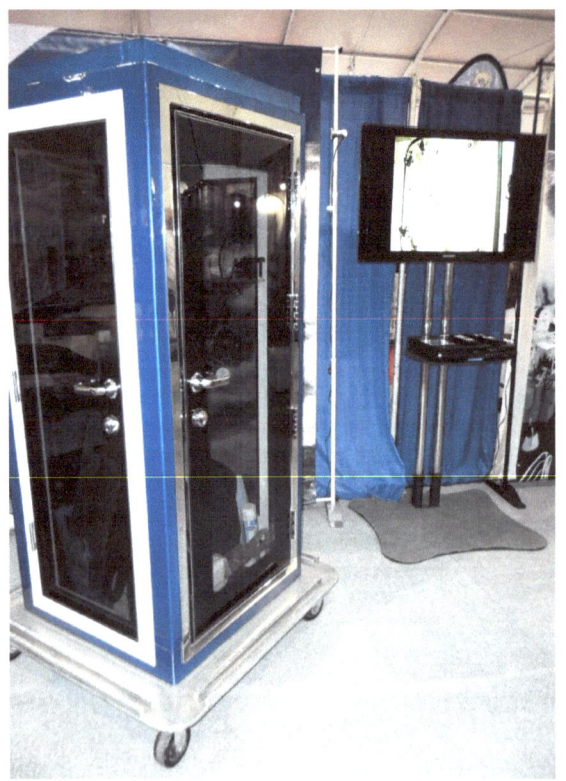

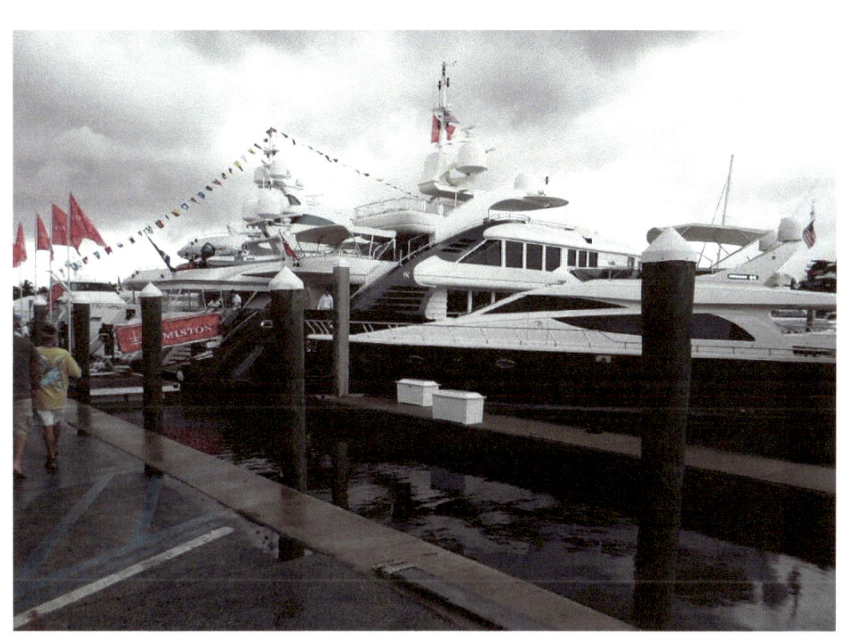

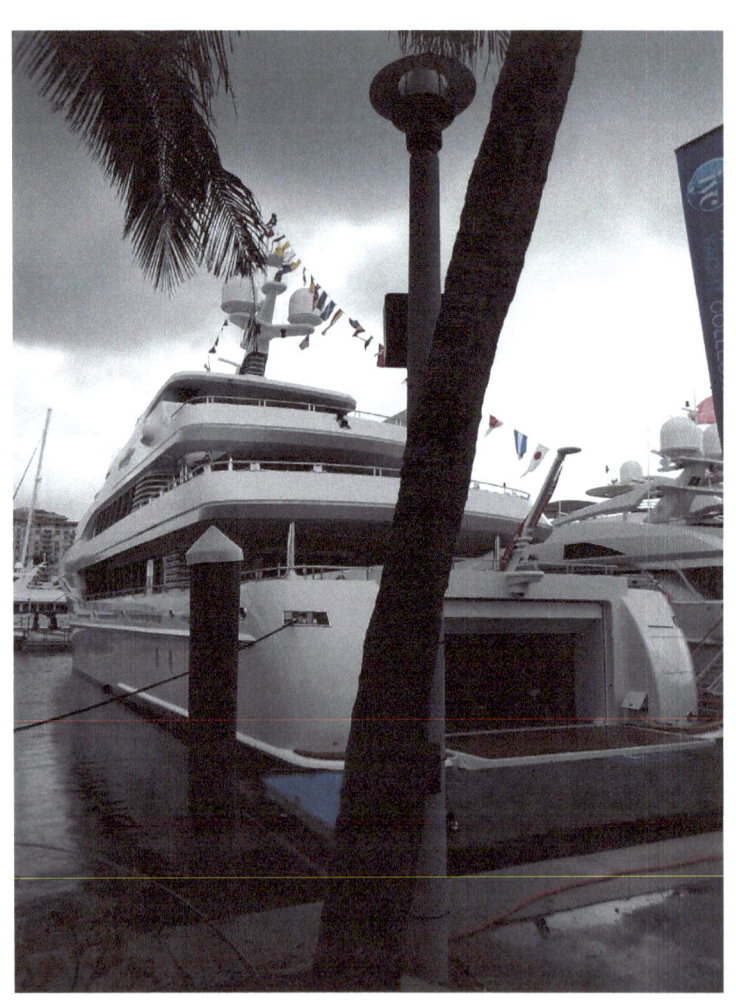

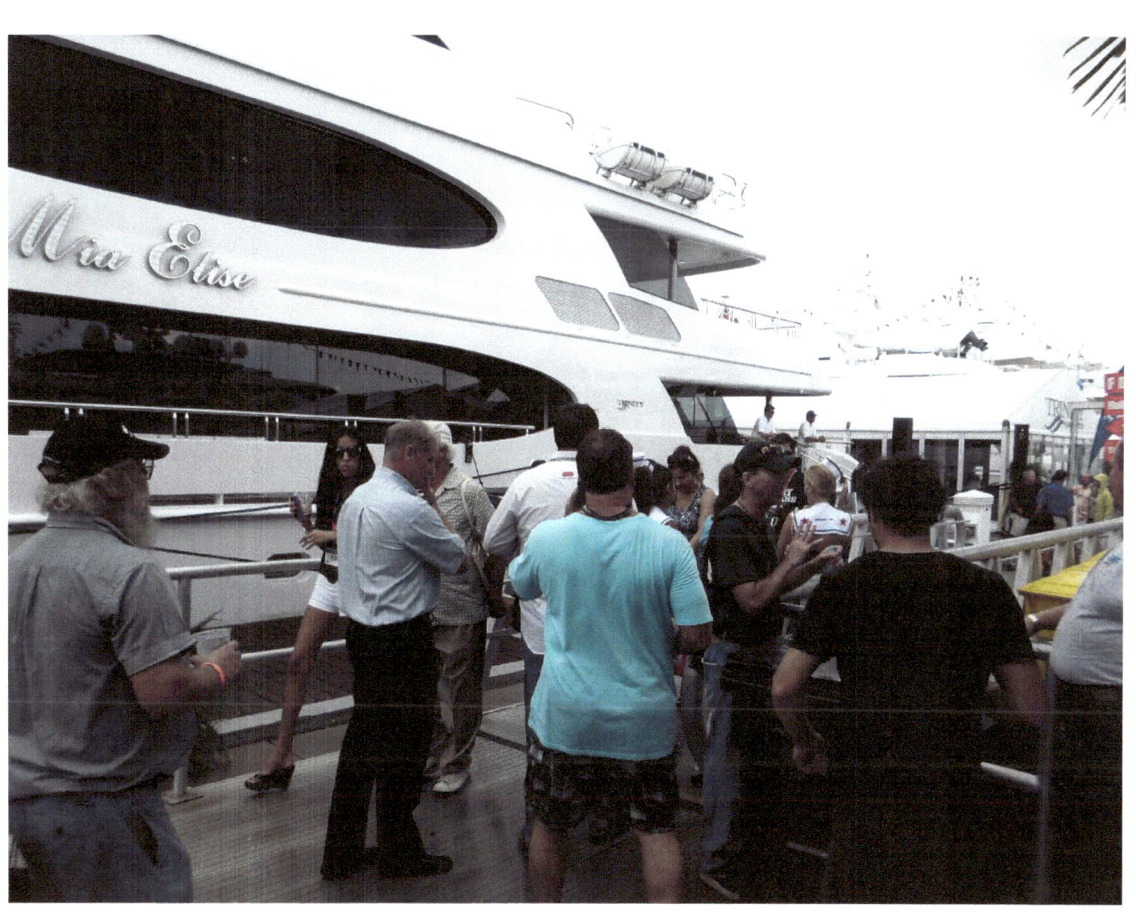

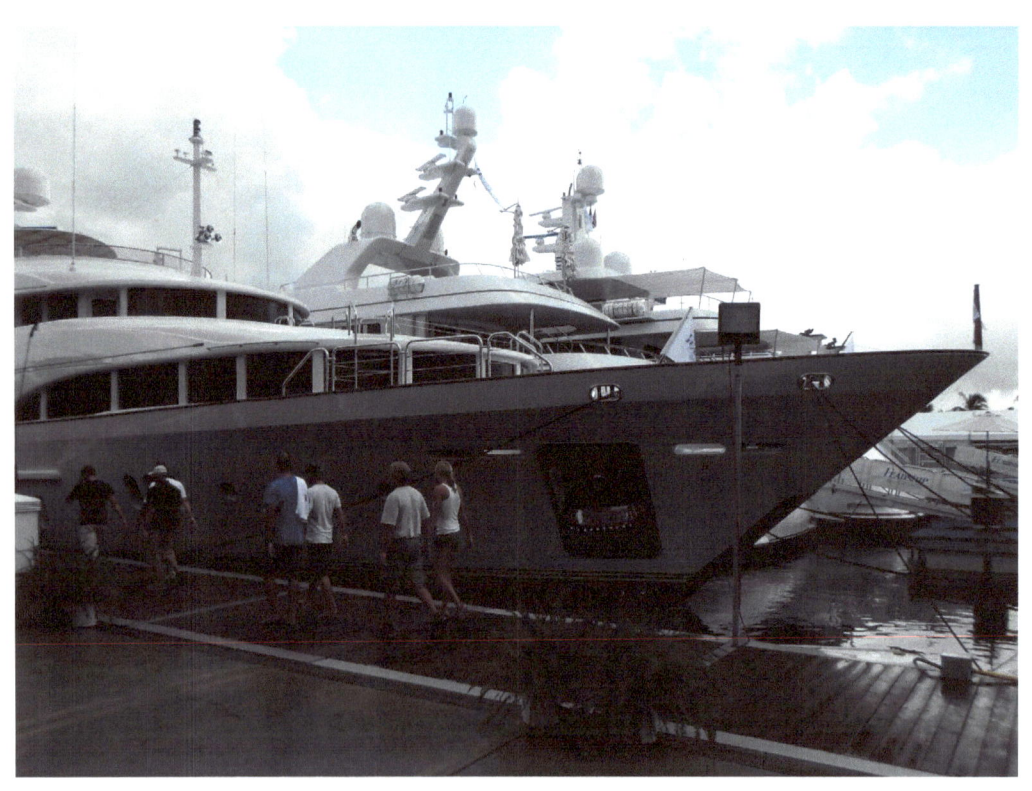

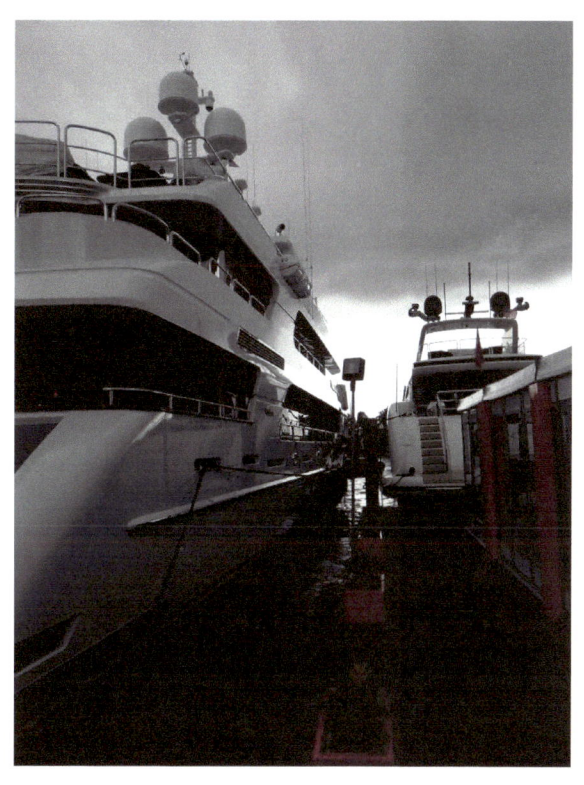

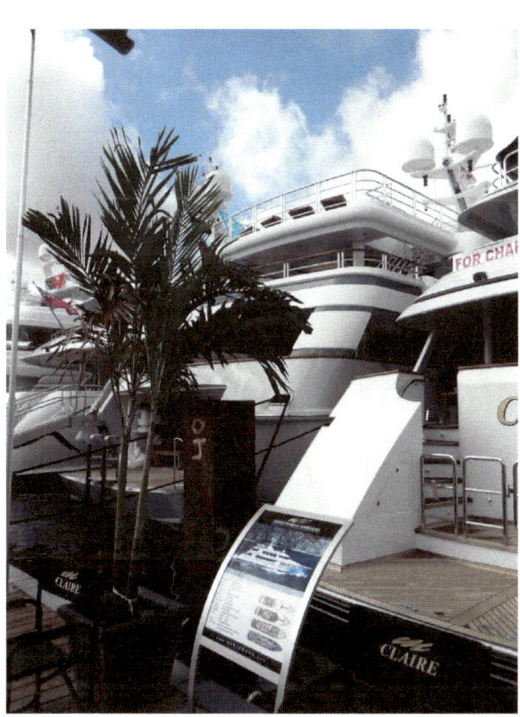

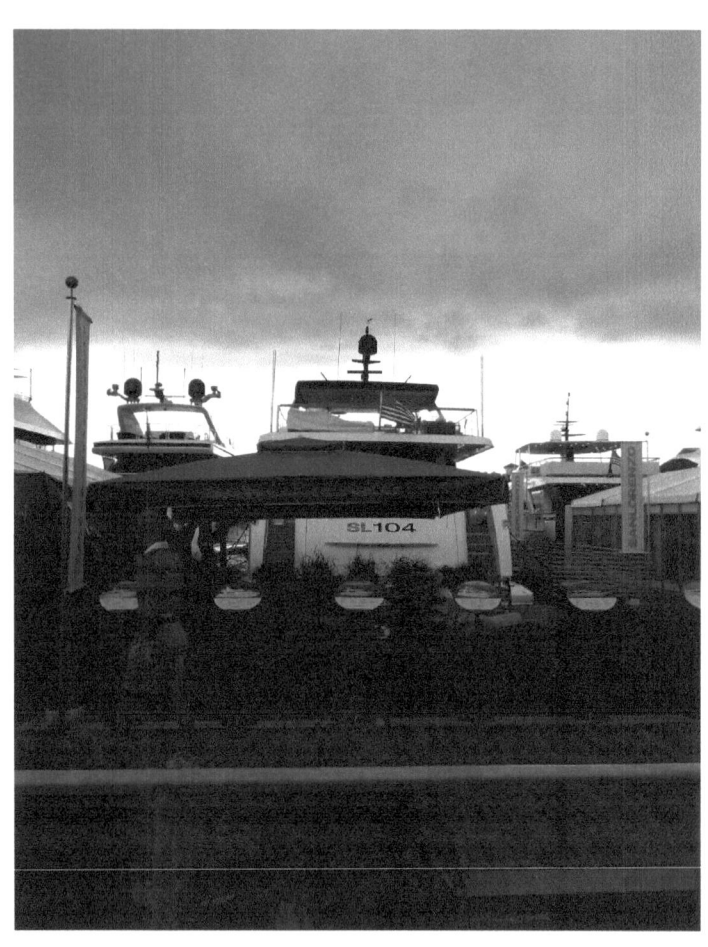

Fort Lauderdale 100
1911-2011

Fort Lauderdale

ort Lauderdale appeared in 1911 with just 175 residents, getting its name from Maj. William Lauderdale, who in 1838, during the Seminole Indian wars built a fort at the mouth of New River. Today, Fort Lauderdale area is full of attractions. Greater Fort Lauderdale's famed beach has changed and offers diverse entertainment. On South Florida's Gold Coast, Greater Fort Lauderdale stretches from Deerfield and Pompano past Fort Lauderdale on the south to Hollywood and Hallandale.

As the "Yachting Capital of the World" it has many yachts docked at the Bahia Mar Yacht Basin and other places. For holiday boat parades the city dresses up big time! County seat Fort Lauderdale, the largest of all, has 150,000 residents and is navigable by its "Venice of America" waterways and also by a grid system of north/south avenues and east/west boulevards. One main-drag exception is the 17th Street Causeway, a major east/west artery that leads over the intracoastal waterway past Port Everglades and curves north onto A1A. The Fort Lauderdale metropolitan Area offers great things to see and to do.

Airboat tours and alligator wrestling await visitors at the 30-acre Everglades Holiday Park at 21940 Griffin Road. At Sawgrass Recreation Park, all sorts of wildlife from snakes and turtles to alligators are on view near an RV park, at 1006 N. U.S. Highway 27 in Weston. In West Lake Park, the Anne Kolb Nature Center has a fishing pier, a five-level observation tower,

two nature trails, and an outdoor amphitheater. An exhibit hall features nature displays, a 10-minute ecologically-themed video and a 3,500-gallon aquarium. Boat tours depart from the nature center dock for 40-minute narrated excursions onto West Lake. The rest of the West Lake Park/Anne Kolb Nature Center complex is a 1,500+ acre offering an abundance of plants and animals, including some threatened species. All these at 751 Sheridan Street, Hollywood.

The Antique Car Museum established to ensure preservation of the Packard Motor Co. history and showcase development of American automotive engineering skills, was founded by Arthur O. Stone, former CEO of Buning the Florist, Inc. The museum collection presents, pre-war models, the Packard and other memorabilia at 1527 Packard (S.W. 1st) Avenue. Greater Fort Lauderdale's beaches -- with 23 miles of sun-drenched shoreline -- are within walking distance of restaurants, hotels and other attractions. On family-oriented Hollywood Beach, jogging and strolling are popular on a 2.5 mile boardwalk. This is also available on Deerfield Beach and Lauderdale-by-the-Sea. Between Hollywood Beach and Dania beach is the pine-shaded John U. Lloyd Beach State Recreation Area, with trails, jetty, marina, and canoeing on Whiskey Creek. Bonnet House was the winter residence of Frederic and Evelyn Bartlett, artists whose taste permeates the breezy two-story home. This 35-acre beachfront estate is named for the bonnet lily once blooming in swamplands. Evelyn loved monkeys and this motif runs throughout. Decor melds with the colony of real Brazilian monkeys outside, to this day adding swinging high notes to weddings and other outdoor celebrations. This estate first belonged to a Chicago lawyer Hugh Taylor Birch, who, arriving in 1893, became enchanted by Fort Lauderdale's untamed coastline. In 1919, his daughter Helen married Bartlett, and Birch gave the property to them for a winter cottage. In 1920, Bonnet House was completed. Soon, Helen died unexpectedly. Bartlett married Evelyn Fortune Lilly in 1931, who wintered at Bonnet House until 1995. Evelyn died at age 109 in Beverly, Mass. two years later. Bonnet House, on the National Register of Historic Places, is a property of the Florida Trust, and is located at 900 North Birch Road. Buehler Planetarium was built in 1965 through a bequest from aviation pioneer Emil Buehler. Today, it is surrounded by palms on the campus of Broward Community College. The planetarium presents shows and astronomical programs; it was renovated with a Zeiss M1015 star projector and computerized automation, and is located at 3501 Southwest Davie Road. In the Butterfly World, on a three-acre outdoor kingdom in northwest Broward's Coconut Creek, winged wonders from the Philippines, Malaysia, South and Central America, and elsewhere are among 80 species, that habitat this tropical rainforest aviary tunnels, observations decks, and waterfalls. There is a museum, insectarium, breeding lab, garden center, and café at 3600 West Sample Road, Coconut Creek.

Dania Antique Row was founded by Danish sellers in an area originally known as Modello. Today, these stores offer different types of furniture, china, glassware, and many shops are housed in historic buildings. A game of the ancient Greeks, Jai-Alai at the Dania Fronton is an offspring of handball. According to the Guinness Book of World Records, It was the Basques, those mysterious people, that polished one-wall handball into the fastest ball game in the world. Dania Jai-Alai features pari-mutuel betting on live jai-alai games, harness racing and horse racing, with bets including Win-Place-Show, Pick 3, Tri-Super, Quiniela, Exacta, Trifecta, and more. All these located at 301 East Dania Beach Boulevard, Dania Beach. The Discovery Bahamas Party Cruise offers dancing with live music, sun decks, swimming pools, cocktail lounges, a Las Vegas-style casino, game rooms, and lots of fun. Leaving Port Everglades at dawn and returning to Fort Lauderdale late in the evening, with an afternoon stop in the Bahamas -- long enough to enjoy tours, shopping, Isle of Capri casino and beaches, is a tour that should not be missed. An Open-air Dolphin Stadium is located on the Broward/Miami-Dade County line. Home to Miami Dolphins football and Florida Marlins baseball, in 1987, it revolutionized pro sports economics by opening Joe

Stadium with Club Level executive suites. In 1990, H. Wayne Huizenga became the point man in bringing major League Baseball to South Florida. In 1994, he took sole stadium ownership. In 1996, Pro Player sponsored the renaming of Joe Robbie to Pro Player. The first football game was a pre-season August 16, 1987 skirmish between the Chicago Bears and the Miami Dolphins. Major League Baseball officially began in South Florida with the spring 1993 Marlin debut.

The Elbo Room was established in 1938 at Las Olas Boulevard and A1A. WWII sailors flocked there in the '40s, followed by decades of Spring Breakers. In 1993, the Elbo was granted the city's first outdoor cafe license. The Evert Tennis Center at Holiday Park has 21 courts. Holiday Park has a baseball/softball field, a football/ soccer field, basketball court, jogging trails, racquetball, shuffleboard, picnic pavilions, children's playground, lighted volleyball, horseshoe pits, and a bicycle path. The park closed midnight to 5 A.M. is located at 701 Northeast 12th Avenue.

On Hillsboro Boulevard, Cove Marina near the Cove Shopping Center has charters for sailfish, kingfish, tuna and more. In Pompano Beach, Pompano Pier extends more than 1,000 feet into the Atlantic and has rod-and-reel rental along with bait. In Lauderdale-by-the-Sea, the 24-hour Anglin's Fishing Pier supplies tackle, bait and a place to fish along with plenty of restaurant atmosphere. The 920-foot Dania Fishing Pier is also open around the clock. Bahia Mar Yacht Basin also has great charter

Southwest 2nd Street) is a 60-acre botanical garden and wildlife sanctuary. It has native and exotic plants, a 200-year-old hammock, citrus groves and Florida "Champion" trees. Also there is a Bird of Prey Center and free-flight walk-through aviary, plus alligators, flamingos and bobcats. Fort Lauderdale Historical Museum has on display artifacts, photographs and other memorabilia from the Seminole period to the present days. Another city museum, Museum of Art Fort Lauderdale is located at One Las Olas Boulevard, in a building that was designed by Edward Larrabee Barnes. Fort Lauderdale Sun Trolley launched in May, 2006, and allows for getting around to attractions via orange and yellow trolleys on routes connecting Las Olas Boulevard, Galt Ocean Mile, Lauderdale Manors, the Courthouse, Tri-Rail, A1A, and more. The Trolleys are operated by the Downtown Fort Lauderdale Transportation Management Association. Gulfstream Park has hosted more than 160 national thoroughbred champions including Holy Bull, Cigar, and Bold Ruler. In 2003, during its 89-day season, Gulfstream marked a Florida pari-mutuel handle record for a single racing meet with $825.3 million. Gulfstream's first racing "season" took place in 1939, and the first day of the meet on Feb. 1 exceeded expectations with a crowd of 18,000 and a mutuel handle of $224,287... Southern Florida's premier horse racing facility, Gulfstream Park offers exciting thoroughbred action, fans flock to this winter horse racing landmark from around the globe. It has massive renovation project that is revolutionary in its scope and amenities. Racing starts in January, and the park also hosts concerts with talent of national renown. All this located at 901 South Federal Highway, Hallandale. For over 60 years, the Jungle Queen has been transporting 14 million guests past eye-popping waterfront homes, historic Stranahan House and other points including the location of the 1836 Cooley family massacre. Cruises depart from the Bahia Mar Yacht Basin daily at 9:30 A.M. and 1:30 P.M., and daily dinner cruises featuring an island variety show and all you-care-to-eat barbecue ribs, chicken and shrimp. The 550 passengers Jungle Queen Riverboat leaves the dock for the 4-hour dinner cruise at 6:00 P.M. daily and sails up the river. A humorous commentary is given by its captain about the sights and homes you'll see. At the exotic island, another home of Jungle Queen, you will be directed to the dining room where barbeque ribs, chicken and shrimp dinner has been prepared. The show will be offered before Jungle Queen leaves the dock for a return trip. The 666-acre Markham Park perched at the edge of the Everglades Conservation Area contains interlocking lakes yielding opportunities for fishing, boating, and a swimming pool complex with mist pool, snack bar, lockers and showers/restrooms. An outdoor target complex includes 50-yard and 100-meter lighted rifle/pistol ranges, lighted skeet/trap fields, a mile-long automated sporting clays course, computerized

5-stand, and a clubhouse. Also on the premises is the Fox Observatory, a model airplane field, and a mountain bike trail. The campground has 86 sites for RV and tent camping. Picnic shelters are available and grills are scattered throughout the park, located at 16001 West State Road 84, Sunrise. At the Museum of Discovery and Science/ Blockbuster 3D IMAX Theater, there are more than 200 hands-on exhibits at this playground of the mind, with eight themed areas: Florida EcoScapes, KidScience, Gizmo City, Space Base, Sound, Choose Health, No Place Like Home and the Traveling Exhibit Hall. The five-story screen of the IMAX Theater showcases a changing schedule of film adventure for family entertainment. It located at 401 Southwest 2nd Street. Pompano Park Harness Track is Florida's only pari-mutuel harness racetrack, and South Florida's only nighttime horse racing facility, ideal for entertainment after a day at the beach, on the golf course, or deep-sea fishing. Guests can also wager on simulcast events and dine at the Top O the Park with a view of the horses and track. Tours are available, at this location of 1800 Southwest 3rd Street, Pompano Beach. Quiet Waters Park offers action that includes Splash Adventure, a high-tech water play system with slides and tunnels. This 430-acre water-oriented park also has a lake for cable waterskiing, and boat rentals. Fishing is permitted on the shores of several lakes. A campground provides pre-setup tents with equipment. Primitive camping is available for nonprofit groups. Quiet Waters also has a large playground, a biking/jogging trail, and a snack bar. It located at 401 South Powerline Road, Deerfield Beach. Downtown Fort Lauderdale's Riverwalk stretches for more than a mile along the historic New River from the Sailboat Bend neighborhood to just short of Stranahan House along the north bank of the New River. Secret Woods Nature Center is a 56-acre Designated Urban Wilderness Area on the south fork of the New River. It opened in 1978 as Broward's first interpretive nature center. The New River Trail, a 3,200-foot, wheelchair-accessible boardwalk, travels through an oak hammock to an overlook on the river, showcasing a brackish-water wetland. The Laurel Oak Trail, a 1,200-foot, wood-chipped trail runs through the drier oak hammock, and an exhibit building has interpretive displays on the nature center's flora and fauna. It is located in Dania Beach. From flea markets to the world's largest outlet mall, Greater Fort Lauderdale has a lot of opportunities for shoppers. Beach Place on Fort Lauderdale Beach has restaurants and a variety of shops and amusements. The Galeria has top brand stores along with 150 specialty shops. Fashionable Las Olas Shopping District is lined with shops and trendy restaurants. West of Andrews Avenue downtown is the Las Olas Riverfront entertainment center with restaurants, shops and a multi-screen theater. As the South's largest flea market, the Fort Lauderdale Swap Shop has many vendors open daily. The Festival Flea Market Mall also has hundreds of shops, booths and kiosks. In Pompano Beach, Pompano Square Mall has approximately 60 shops and department stores. In Sunrise, the alligator-shaped Sawgrass Mills, ranks only behind Disney as the second biggest tourist draw in Florida, with more than 400 retail outlets and name-brand discounters. Stranahan house is now a museum. This turn-of-the-century structure nestled among downtown skyscrapers was the New River home of Fort Lauderdale's first school teacher, Ivy Cromartie Stranahan. Her husband Frank ran a trading post, doing business with the Seminoles at the turn of the century. Despondent over ravages of the hurricane of '26 and the market crash of '29, Stranahan did himself in by tying a weight to his leg and jumping into the river. Ivy lived in the house until her death in 1971. This vernacular style building, also has been a post office, bank and town hall. It still showcases Ivy's blue and white china and pictures of Old Fort Lauderdale on tours, by guides in turn-of-the-century costume that last an hour, located at Las Olas Boulevard at Southeast Sixth Avenue. The Water Taxi/Water Bus provides a scenic alternative for accessing attractions, hotels, restaurants and other places. Water Taxi / Water Bus, serves the community as a designated driver and offers an all-day pass.

Much more is waiting to be discovered.

About Photographer

*N*adia Russ (aka Nadejda Maloletneva) was born in the Ukrainian town of Konotop, into a professional military officer's family. Her father, Ivan was born and studied military science in the Moscow region, in Russia, and later, with Vera, Nadia's mother, traveled nationally on a Mission. Ivan loved the Ukrainian nature, and after he retired in 1958 from the Soviet Army (he was then 34 years old), they settled down in the Ukrainian town of Konotop. Nadia was born a year later, in 1959, and spent her childhood in Konotop, but always dreamed about moving to Moscow. It is in Ukraine, that she began studying visual arts from famous masters of the past through art books and reproductions, which her mother Vera was collecting in their home. Vera was a big fan of the visual arts and literature, and their home was always full of excitement and adoration related to the visual arts, old and contemporary masters whose pieces were the source of inspiration. Nadia daily heard about and saw the reproductions of works of Leonardo da Vinci, Michelangelo, Rafael, contemporary Russian artists such as Petrov-Vodkin and others. Her passionate love for the visual arts came not only from her mother, but also her father, who was creative and talented in visual arts.

In 1976, Nadia left Konotop for Kursk, where she studied music and pedagogy in college. After her graduation from college, in 1979, Nadia moved to Moscow, where she experimented with different spheres of creativity. There, she made many friends, and among them was Zita Sovdagarova, a talented and very progressive Armenian woman, psychologist, who was Nadia's inspiration in journalism (then, Nadia was interviewing Russian congressmen for two national publications, in 1989-1992); Yuri Petrosian, sculptor, member of Moscow Union of Artists, who was subletting Nadia an art studio in the center of Moscow; Fira, who was a former ballet movie director in Russian television and a walking inspiration; and many others.

Nadia Russ began painting seriously in 1989, during the perestroika period, when Russians were gradually moving out of the "swamp," created by communist's ideology. A few months later, she was participating with her ink drawings in her first group an art exhibition in the legendary *Moscow's Manege*.

In 1992, Nadia visited New York City and successfully exhibited her work there. In 1996-2000, she resided in the Bahamas where she began using water paints exclusively, such as acrylic, and said "good bye" to oil forever. Then, in 1996, she was first and the only Russian resident in this sunny and exotic island country where her work gained its brightness. Also, there, she got her pseudonym to her original 'Nadejda Maloletneva', which was easier to pronounce -- 'Nadia Russ'. In 2000-2001, in *Xanadu* hotel, she operated her *Art Gallery Club 13*.

In 2000, she moved to the United States, where she lives up until the present. In 2003, Nadia Russ manifested *NeoPopRealism*, a new visual arts style which combines the brightness and simplicity of *Pop Art* with depth of *realism*. Her canvases, drawings and glass pieces are in private, public and corporate collections worldwide, in permanent collections of several museums such as *Ukrainian Museum* in New York City (USA), *MOYA* - Museum of Young Art in Vienna (Austria), Sumy and Simferopol Art Museums in Ukraine, *WEAM* - World Erotic Art Museum in Miami (USA), Lebedyn and Konotop Art Museums in Ukraine, Historical Museum of Fort Lauderdale (USA), D. Burliuk Foundation in Ukraine, and others. In 2008 - 2010 Nadia Russ founded and juried the *NeoPopRealism Starz International* art competitions. In 2009-2011, she authored the art related books -- "*NeoPopRealism Starz*" two volumes and "*NEW MILLENNIUM ART.*" Nadia Russ is founder of the *NeoPopRealism Journal* & *Wonderpedia* publications online, dedicated to arts, culture, books, celebrities and news. She lives in New York City and Florida.

О Фотографе

Надя Русс (иначе Надежда Малолетнева) родилась в украинском городе Конотопе, в семье профессионального военного. Ее отец, Иван, родившийся и изучавший военное дело в подмосковье, позже, с Верой, матерью Нади, путешествовал по России с миссией. Ивану нравилась украинская природа и после того, как он ушел в отставку в 1958 (ему тогда было 34 года), они осели в украинском живописном городе Конотопе. Надя родилась год спустя, в 1959, и провела ее детство в Конотопе, но мечтала о переезде в Москву. На Украине она начала изучать изобразительные искусства, произведения известных мастеров прошлого через художественные книги и репродукции, которые ее мать Вера коллекционировала. Вера была большим любителем изобразительных искусств и литературы, и их дом всегда был полон обожания, связанного с произведениями мастеров прошлого и настоящего, источниками вдохновения: работами Леонардо да Винчи, Микеланджело, Рафаэля, современных российских художников -- Петрова-Водкина и других. Надя ежедневно слышала о них и видела репродукции их работ. Ее страстная любовь к изобразительным искусствам передалась ей не только от ее матери, но также от отца, который был творческим и талантливым в изобразительных искусствах человеком.

В 1976, Надя переехала в Курск, где она изучала музыку и педагогику в колледже. После его окончания, в 1979, она переехала в Москву, где экспериментировала в различных областях, базируясь на ее творческом потенциале. Там, она обрела много друзей, и среди них была Зита Совдагарова, талантливая и очень прогрессивная армянская женщина, психолог, которая была вдохновением Надиному увлечению журналистикой. Тогда (1989-1992), Надя брала интервьюировала Депутатов Верховного Совета, таких как Рой Медведев, Анатолий Денисов, А. Казанник для двух журналов национального значения, и была награждена призом журналистов. Юрий Петросян, скульптор, член Московского Союза Художников, передавал Наде в субаренду художественную студию в центре Москвы; Фира, бывший директор фильмов о балете на Российском телевидении, была ходячим вдохновением Надиных новых проектов..., многие другие.

Надя Русс серьезно начала заниматься изобразительным искусством в 1989, во время перестройки. Несколько месяцев спустя, она участвовала с ее рисунками тушью в ее первой групповой художественной выставке в легендарном Московском Манеже.

In 1992, она посетила Нью-Йорк и успешно выставила там ее работы. В 1996-2000, она жила на Багамах, где начала работать исключительно водными красками -- акриловыми. Тогда, в 1996, Надя Русс была первым российским жителем на Багамах, этих солнечных и экзотичных островах. Ее работы обрели яркость; также, там она взяла ее псевдоним 'Nadia Russ', который было легче произнести. В 2000-2001, там, в гостинице Занаду она организовала и управляла ее галереей "Художественный Клуб Галерея 13".

В 2000, Надя Русс ереехала в Соединенные Штаты, где она живет и сейчас. В 2003, она объявила NeoPopRealism, новый стиль в изобразительном искусстве, который соединяет в себя яркость и простоту Поп Арта с глубиной реализма. Ее холсты, рисунки и стекло находятся в коллекциях по всему миру, включая постоянные собрания нескольких музеев: украинского Музея в Нью-Йорке (США), MOYA - Музей Молодого Искусства в Вене (Австрия), Сумской и Симферопольский Художественные Музеи на Украине, WEAM - Мировой Эротический Художественный Музей в Майами (США), Лебединский и Конотопский Художественные Музеи на Украине, Исторический Музей Форт-Лодердейла (США), Фонд Д. Бурлюка на Украине, и т.д. В 2008 - 2010 Надя Русс основала и судила NeoPopRealism Starz Международный художественный конкурс. В 2009-2011 она издала несколько книг об искусстве -- "NeoPopRealism Starz", "NEW MILLENNIUM ART", etc. Надя Русс (Надежда Малолетнева) основатель журналов онлайн NeoPopRealism (2007-) и Wonderedia (2008-), посвященных искусству, культуре, книгам, знаменитостям, новостям. В настоящее время она живет в Нью-Йорке и Флориде.

First Edition

11 12 13 14 15   1 2 3 4 5 6 7 8 9 10

Published by
NeoPopRealism Press
P.O. Box 366
New York, NY 10013

neopoprealism.org
NeopoprealismPress@mail.com

Designed by Nadia RUSS
Written in English with partial translation in Russian

Printed in the United States of America

RUSS, NADIA
Fort Lauderdale 100: Yachting Capital
A Must-Have Collector's Edition

100 photographs of Fort Lauderdale
by Nadia RUSS

Foreword by Mayor of the City of Fort Lauderdale John P. "Jack" SEILER

ISBN-13: 9780615562223
ISBN-10: 0615562221

This third volume "Yachting Catital" of the book "Fort Lauderdale 100: A Must-Have Collector's Edition" is dedicated to 100-year anniversary of the City of Fort Lauderdale.

First volume of "Fort Lauderdale 100: A Must-Have Collector's Edition", ISBN: 9780615470085, published by NeoPopRealism PRESS April 15, 2011.
Second volume of "Fort Lauderdale 100: REFLECTIONS: A Must-Have Collector's Edition", ISBN: 9780615554464, published by NeoPopRealism PRESS October 15, 2011.

NeoPopRealism canons for happier life:

 1. Be beautiful; 2. Be creative and productive; never stop studying & learning; 3. Be peace-loving, positive-minded; 4. Do not accept communist or any totalitarian and destructive philosophy; 5. Be free-minded, do the best you can to move the world to peace and harmony; 6. Be family oriented, self-disciplined; 7. Be free spirited. Follow your dreams, if they are not destructive, but constructive; 8. Believe in god. God is one, it is harmony and striving for perfection; 9. Be supportive to those who need you, be generous; 10. Create your life as a great adventurous story.

NeoPopRealism 10 canons created by artist Nadia Russ in 2004.

www.ingramcontent.com/pod-product-compliance
Lightning Source LLC
Chambersburg PA
CBHW051020180526
45172CB00002B/417